Gigolos

The Secret Lives of Men who Service Women

Dane Taylor & Antonia Newton-West

Commentary by
Danielle Merlan, Ph.D.

MT. IVY PRESS ▲ PO BOX 142 ▲ BOSTON MA 02258

First Edition Published 1994

Design: BECKdesigns

Cover photo: David Henderson
              Eric Roth Photography

Cover "jewels": N Landau Hyman

Cover printing: Henry N. Sawyer Company
                Charlestown, MA

Library of Congress Card Catalog Number
94-076930

Mt. Ivy Press, Inc.
P.O. Box 142
Boston, MA 02258

Gigolos

The Secret Lives of Men who Service Women

Dane Taylor & Antonia Newton-West

Commentary by
Danielle Merlan, Ph.D.

MT. IVY PRESS ▲ PO BOX 142 ▲ BOSTON MA 02258

The Gigolo in the Nineties —
Seeking Out the Invisible Man

Look in the personals section of any alternative newspaper anywhere in the country and you'll see them. They're different from the usual "boy seeks girl" ad; you can spot them by the code language and format. For instance, the ad usually stresses that the man is young and attractive. He may describe himself as "virile" or "masculine" and make some allusion to his interest in pleasing a woman sexually. The ad often mentions that he is "discreet." The tip-off is that the advertiser does not specify the qualities he seeks in a woman: Her age may be "35 to 60", her "marital status and race not important." Her appearance is never mentioned at all. Generally, he only requires that she be "financially secure" or "generous." When you see an ad that more or less matches this description it's a good bet the advertiser is a man who services women for money.

In researching this book, the authors answered ads like this in several major cities across the country. They also placed their own ads "seeking paid escorts for research in connection with a publication." (What astonished them was the number of men who called wanting to know how to get into the gigolo business!) In addition, they contacted people referred by the interviewees. They had no difficulty locating men in the business of servicing women. Almost half were willing to be interviewed but only if their anonymity were assured. More difficult was finding women to talk about their experiences with these men. Even with a promise of anonymity, few women were willing to be interviewed.

The people who place ads and answer them are undoubtedly just the tip of the iceberg. There's no telling how many men today are in relationships with women that, though informal, technically would qualify them as "kept men." Since there are no studies available, anecdotal evidence must suffice. To that end, the authors have done informal polling on their own, chatting with people on their perceptions about the topic, gigolos. What they learned was intriguing.

For instance, women as a group were rarely surprised at the idea of gigolos being around today. Many of them had a story to tell of their own. One woman exclaimed, "Why, I know three gigolos. I'm sixty years old so you know I understand what that word means!" Another woman stated matter-of-factly, "My brother's a gigolo. He's thirty-six, and he's never worked in his life. He always picks women who support him. He finally married one — a lawyer." Another woman who was independently wealthy said that she had supported a man whom she considered "essentially a gigolo" for several years. "He fit the picture perfectly. He claimed to be of noble descent, was very smooth and charming and an elegant dresser. And, of course, he had no money."

Another woman told this story: "My husband and I used to vacation in the Caribbean a lot. After a few days at the resort, we would notice each batch of new tourists as they arrived. Often at dinner we would see one or two women who had just checked in that afternoon already seated with a gorgeous native hunk. These guys were with them for their whole vacations; we'd see them going together to all the sights and activities. We wondered how they met these fellas so fast, and then someone told us that they were paid escorts."

What is particularly intriguing about this survey is the reaction of men to the subject of gigolos. One prominent attorney who was asked how he felt about gigolos grinned: "Nice work if you can get it." Another professional man inquired, "Where do I sign up?" That reaction was typical. "Nice" men — doctors, business owners, professors, fathers, even grandfathers — were fascinated and titillated by the subject. If ever there was a stigma in men's minds attached to the word "gigolo" it seems to be nonexistent today.

Of course, their female cohorts would be highly offended if anyone suggested that they might like to become paid escorts. The difference seems to be that women are acutely aware of the deep and degrading stigma associated with female prostitution. Men, never having felt the sting of that lash, see as a compliment a woman's willingness to pay for their time and services. They perceive the issue this way: "Not only does she find me attractive, she is so attracted to me that she'll even pay for me."

Gigolos are making a silent comeback for the first time since they debuted in America more than a half century ago. The authors of this book set out to find the answers to the question, "Why?"

At their request, some factual details contained in all the following interviews have been altered to protect the identity of the subjects with the exception of Attorney Bielitz's.

Albert Bielitz, Jr. Esq.

Albert Bielitz is a prominent criminal defense attorney in Boston whose practice concentrates on sex-related crimes. He represents the largest escort service on the East Coast.

Toni: Do you mind us using your name in the book?

Attorney Bielitz: It's up to you. I wouldn't be in any trouble. Fire away.

Toni: Can you explain a little bit about what the laws are regarding escorts?

Attorney Bielitz: OK. It's in fact the same for a male escort as it is for a female escort in Massachusetts. And the law sees escorting as a business engaged in sex for hire or sale.

Basically, the law looks at it as a form of prostitution. It is illegal.

Dane: And male escorts fall into that category?

Attorney Bielitz: Yes, they do. If you're in it, you're committing a crime.

Dane: What are the penalties?

Attorney Bielitz: It depends. It's a whole gamut, a wide range of sentences and fines.

Dane: Are there many convictions involving male escorts?

Attorney Bielitz: No. I don't know of one.

Toni: OK. If it's not legal to be a male escort or a prostitute, is it legal to operate a male escort agency?

Attorney Bielitz: Well, it's legal to operate an escort agency. As long as the escort agency isn't involved in prostitution, that is. And if you operate an agency that is involved in prostitution, there's a mandatory two-year prison sentence if you get busted for deriving support from prostitution.

Toni: Do the laws vary from state to state?

Attorney Bielitz: Yes. Dramatically.

Dane: We understand that you represent some people who own or operate escort agencies.

Attorney Bielitz: Quite a few.

Toni: Are they generally catering to women or catering to men?

Attorney Bielitz: Both. Everything under the sun.

Dane: Do you represent companies that are just in Massachusetts?

Attorney Bielitz: No. Connecticut, New Hampshire, Vermont, Rhode Island, Maine, Massachusetts.

Dane: How do agencies protect themselves from prosecution?

Attorney Bielitz: Well, when you go to work for them, they have you sign their documents saying there will be no drugs, no alcohol, no sex in order to shift the liability to the escort. If an arrest is made, the agency will say, "We don't know anything about this." And they're covered because of the document that was signed. All the escort agencies do this; it's pretty much standard procedure.

Toni: So if a woman calls up and asks for a male escort, and then sex is involved and the exchange of money, the individual would be prosecuted? Not the agency?

Attorney Bielitz: Right. What normally happens is that the cops will get a policewoman to go undercover and pose as a customer. After the date, she gives an affidavit and the police get a search warrant and go to the headquarters where the agency is set up and seize all the records. They'll build the case from there.

Toni: How heavily are the police involved in the agencies?

Attorney Bielitz: I represent the largest escort service on the East Coast. Their biggest clients are the United States Federal Marshall Service and the State Department. I wonder if that will shock your readers.

Dane: Al, do the same people run agencies from state to state?

Attorney Bielitz: Well, they're not necessarily the same people, but the agencies all seem to be interconnected. They all know each other. They send the guys and girls up here from Miami, then they go from here to New York. And this is not organized crime either.

Toni: With most agencies, do you know how they have it set up as far as splitting an escort's fee?

Attorney Bielitz: Depends on each agency.

Toni: Is there a standard in the business?

Attorney Bielitz: No, but the competition is what determines its standard. The agencies I've represented have charged 40 percent. The escort takes home 60 percent.

Dane: Of the agencies you represent, how long has the oldest one been around?

Attorney Bielitz: Like forever. Fifteen years.

Toni: How big are they?

Attorney Bielitz: Huge.

Toni: How many guys do they have working?

Attorney Bielitz: One hundred and fifty.

Toni: Is it as dirty a business as people seem to think or is that a misconception?

Attorney Bielitz: It depends. It can be filthy, it can be wild, and it can be extremely profitable.

Dane: What type of people are working as escorts?

Attorney Bielitz: The big one that I represent has teachers, secretaries, probation officers, police officers, executive vice presidents of major banks, a president of a Chamber of Commerce.

Toni: These are people who are working as escorts??

Attorney Bielitz: Yes, they are working as escorts.

Toni: Now, it's not illegal to advertise as an escort, right?

Attorney Bielitz: No. Let's be clear. Escorting is not illegal. Prostitution is. Escorting someone to an event is perfectly legal. The sexual activity is what's illegal.

Toni: Let's say I reach for the phone and call an escort agency. They send over Steven. It turns out I don't want him for just dinner. I want him overnight. OK, the police come in. We're busted. What happens to me? I'm the woman who hired him.

Attorney Bielitz: Probably nothing. They can arrest you under the "john law." It's usually a hundred dollar fine. They can arrest you; they usually don't.

Dane: They arrest the person that's prostituting?

Attorney Bielitz: Right.

Toni: Wait a minute. Just what is entrapment? I mean, if you're the escort and someone comes to you and makes a deal to have sex...

Attorney Bielitz: Let's say I'm trying to get the escort. I say, "I want to have sex. How much is it?" As soon as you say "three hundred dollars," you're under arrest.

Toni: But what if during the transaction, the escort asks, "Are you a cop?"

Attorney Bielitz: Doesn't mean anything. I may be a cop. I can say no.

Dane: Really? Doesn't that constitute entrapment?

Attorney Bielitz: No. That's a huge misconception. Doesn't mean crap. Let me tell you about one case I had. A girl in a massage parlor.

She says, "Are you a police officer?"

He says, "Absolutely not. Do I look like a cop?" So they make the deal, then, boom! — he arrests her.

She says, "You can't do that!"

He says, "Since when? You're busted."

So you see, that's a very dangerous misconception that these escorts have out there. They don't realize what the laws are.

Toni: So then what specifically is entrapment?

Attorney Bielitz: Entrapment is getting someone to do something that they would not normally do. For example, you're not a coke dealer. So I come up to you and I say, "Toni, I'll give you twenty thousand dollars to deliver this package of coke across the state." Now, you didn't approach me. I approached you. That's entrapment.

Dane: What happens if a person gets arrested on a prostitution charge?

Attorney Bielitz: Continue without a finding. Fifty dollar court costs, one hundred dollar court costs.

Dane: Second time you get arrested?

Attorney Bielitz: Two hundred dollar court costs. Third time, it's suspended sentence and a fine.

Toni: When do you go to jail?

Attorney Bielitz: Eventually.

Dane: So you can go on like it's a pretty safe business, huh?

Attorney Bielitz: In truth, yes. And if you have a good lawyer, you don't ever have to lose sleep.

Dane: Do you think Boston has a bigger scene in this business than Miami or Ft. Lauderdale?

Attorney Bielitz: I think it would have to be bigger than Miami or Lauderdale. And it's getting bigger every year.

Dane: Do people ever call up an escort and really just want a date, no sex? And still pay three hundred dollars or something just for a date with that person?

Attorney Bielitz: Sure, there's a lot of that going on. I mean, hiring a guy from an escort service doesn't necessarily mean you're going to have sex every time. That's what everybody thinks and, normally, I think that's what goes on, but sometimes it's just a date.

For example, let's say you're a famous actor and you call up an escort service to have an escort go with you to a party. The odds are that you're doing it so some girl doesn't try to pick you up and accuse you of rape later. As a celebrity, you're always vulnerable to extortion attempts.

Toni: Is that fairly common?

Attorney Bielitz: You mean people hiring escorts for protection? Very common.

Let me put it this way. If Mike Tyson had done that, he wouldn't have gone to jail.

Dane: What does someone pay for an escort just to accompany them?

Attorney Bielitz: It's normally around two hundred or three hundred dollars for an escort just to go out with someone. Sometimes sex will be expected; sometimes it won't. I know of an instance where a guy made fifteen thousand dollars for a week just to keep a certain actress company while she was here in Boston. There are huge amounts of money one can make.

Toni: If prostitution is illegal, how come being a kept woman is not? You're still getting paid in terms of gifts, cash, and they're paying your livelihood?

Attorney Bielitz: Well, why isn't marriage illegal then?

Toni: But you do see an inconsistency there?

Attorney Bielitz: Yes.

Toni: So why don't escorts just say, when they're being arrested, "I was a kept man! I'm not a prostitute."

Attorney Bielitz: Maybe they could. They just haven't bothered to try.

Toni: What about certain types of sexual acts? Are the acts themselves illegal?

Attorney Bielitz: The laws vary from state to state. For example, oral sex and anal sex are illegal in some states, including Massachusetts.

Dane: Are strip clubs legal?

Attorney Bielitz: Yep.

Dane: What about some of these sex clubs?

Attorney Bielitz: Illegal.

Toni: The sex clubs where they're not actually having sex but the dominatrixes are cracking their whips, is that illegal? Where does something like that fall? I mean, it's not sex.

Attorney Bielitz: That's what the question is.

Toni: So the law might see it as an unnatural act?

Attorney Bielitz: But what's unnatural if nobody is injuring anybody? It's not cut-and-dried. It's a legal question.

Dane: Is cocaine prevalent in the escort business?

Attorney Bielitz: It's very prevalent among the people that are involved in the business. Most of the people who own the businesses, though, are trying to keep the coke out of it. The risk is too high.

Dane: What kind of people run the agencies?

Attorney Bielitz: They're tough. They're serious. I mean, you've got these huge agencies that are really a business. And they prove that they are. They have accountants. They pay taxes. They provide drivers. They provide protection, the works.

And the escorts, they're not dummies either. These are people who speak foreign languages. They're well educated. In one of the agencies I represent, a male escort is in law school right now, another is in his last year of medical school, another is doing his residency. This guy could be taking out your appendix in a couple of years.

Dane: With the agencies you represent, what type of people are calling escorts?

Attorney Bielitz: The client lists are ungodly. I mean the people using escorts are often very prominent: doctors, lawyers, politicians, women who run their own businesses. It's just unreal. It's a different world. Virtually anything goes.

Toni: Would you personally like to see prostitution legalized?

Attorney Bielitz: It should be.

Toni: It would take away some business from you, though, wouldn't it?

Attorney Bielitz: I got enough.

Dane: In a normal issue of the *Boston Phoenix*, how many ads in the personals are undercover plants?

Attorney Bielitz: Ten, fifteen.

Dane: Are you astute enough to pick them out?

Attorney Bielitz: Sometimes I can. It's interesting, too, because the *Phoenix* is really growing. The personal section is huge and expanding all

Gigolos • 9

the time.

Toni: Do you think men make more money than women in this business?

Attorney Bielitz: Yes. Definitely.

Toni: Why is that?

Attorney Bielitz: Because there aren't enough of them doing this.

Dane: Why do you think that is?

Attorney Bielitz: I don't know. Here in Boston there just aren't enough male escorts for the demand. It's funny, really. You're talking about a very, very conservative area, yet it's filled with wild women with too much money who want a lot of sex. I suppose that will change, though, in a few years, as more men come up here. But right now, there aren't enough guys. It's a seller's market right now, ripe for the picking.

The American Gigolo: Bellwether of women's changing role in society

The gigolo in America is a twentieth-century phenomenon. Defined in 1922 by Edna Ferber as "a man who lives off women's money," his appearance on the American scene in the early part of this century coincides with a revolution in women's role in society. The first gigolos literally danced into view, for they arrived in step with a new dance craze: the tango. In fact, the word "gigolo" derives from the French word for dance partner.

Born vulgar and suggestive in the streets of Buenos Aires, the tango quickly made it to the Continent where sophisticated Parisians polished its steps and gestures creating an elegant, highly erotic set of movements. When the tango arrived on the American shore, it was met by a population who were in the throes of completely redefining themselves.

America was in a period of massive social and economic upheaval, shifting from a rural, agrarian society to an urban, industrial one. The middle class was rapidly expanding and a new breed of woman was emerging, one who was educated, who had free time and extra money, one who was intensely curious about the world outside her traditional sphere of domesticity.

The Woman's Suffrage Movement had been gaining strength for almost forty years, growing more militant than when Susan B. Anthony began the crusade for women's voting rights in 1869. Women in the early part of the century took to the streets by the thousands, and even chained themselves to the White House fence, to protest a political system that was the exclusive province of men. Young women who flaunted their disdain for conventional dress, behavior and moral values were known as "flappers." In the climate of social turbulence leading up to the First World War, women threw away their corsets, cut their hair and flocked to the cabarets to dance the tango.

There they were greeted by eager playmates, the "gigolos" (or "lounge lizards" or "taxi dancers" as they were also called), young men who hung around the clubs looking for women willing to pay for their skills on the dance floor. While husbands attended to business or other women, lonely or bored ladies could find easy diversion dancing the tango in the arms of a dashing stranger.

Women adored these seedily dapper young men, many of them recent immigrants from Greece, Russia, Italy or France, because they affected refined manners, portraying themselves as sophisticated and worldly. Ferber described them as, "Lean, sallow, handsome, expert, and unwholesome, one saw them everywhere, their slim waists and sleek heads in juxtaposition to plump, respectable American matrons and slender, respectable American flappers."

Not insignificant in the gigolos' appeal was their sultry sexuality. "To the dismay of moralists, men and women in the tango even brought legs and pelvic regions into intimate contact in the much feared dip portion of the dance, which placed women in a horizontal position reeking of sexual exploration and subjugation," wrote Lewis A. Erenberg in *Steppin' Out*, an examination of New York night life of the time. New York clubs like Maxim's, Delmonico's and the Ritz Grill played host to scores of women eager to pay a gigolo or taxi dancer to glide her across the floor and murmur sweet flatteries in her ear, flirtations which she might, if she chose, turn into something more.

In 1914, at the height of the dance craze, world war broke out and America shipped its young men abroad to fight. American women went into the labor force or undertook volunteer activities outside the home to support the war effort. At night, unescorted women frequented the cabarets spending money they had earned themselves or gleaned from their absent husbands' funds.

The gigolos capitalized on their appeal as exotic foreigners though, in reality, they often hailed from a background of poverty and had no education, no skills and little English. Their posturing, flattering and expert dancing enabled them to earn enough fees and tips, and often more, to survive.

The war ended in 1918 and two years later women won the right to vote. In 1922 the first woman was elected to the Senate and the Equal Rights Amendment was introduced the following year. Following the war and well into the "Roaring Twenties," American women proclaimed their independence. It was a "period when women went about conspicuously asserting the right to their own enjoyment of life."

In the boom years after the war, social restrictions continued to unravel. Women embraced drinking and smoking as activities that signaled that they indeed had "come a long way, baby." Meanwhile, the mad whirl of cabaret life continued unabated. In that arena, for the first time in American history, women were getting from men what they wanted, on their own terms. Writing at the time, Edna Ferber in her short story, Gigolo, describes a scene in which a mother and daughter size up an attractive gigolo and the daughter asks her father to "Get that one Dad, will you, if you can? You dance with him first, Mother and then I'll —" Ferber regarded with contempt, the "incredible and pathetic male creatures,...who, for ten francs...would dance with any woman wishing to dance."

Yet the ladies who patronized the clubs reveled in their new-found independence and the exhilaration of being in control. "There were many establishments where she paid such partners for dancing with her, dismissing them if they displeased her, and if she left the dance floor for the casual hotel bedroom, the choice again was hers."

One of the most notorious gigolos of the twenties was an Italian immigrant. Mysterious, suave and smoldering, this nineteen-year-old farm lad became a favorite of the ladies at Maxim's. They showered him with expensive gifts and big tips for his dancing skills and his ability to "put almost any woman at ease and make her seem more beautiful and graceful than she actually was." In a very short time, he went from two-bit cabaret dancer to partnering Bonnie Glass, a famous exhibition dancer of that era. The next stop for him was Hollywood where he was nicknamed "The Red Hot Lover." His name — Rudolph Valentino.

In his biography *Valentino*, Irving Shulman says that the most famous and idolized leading man of his time felt that "in their emancipation they [women] used him, as a commodity, to be bought, exchanged or discarded at whim."

Valentino died in 1926 at the age of thirty-one. Three years later, the era of high times and fast living died too, killed instantly by the crash of the stock market. The Roaring Twenties passed into memory.

The Depression had a particularly disastrous effect on women's economic independence. By 1940 the number of women holding jobs fell to 1910 levels. Women would not for half a century regain the kind of power they had held in the cabaret years.

Glen

Glen contacted us through an ad we had placed. Like most of the escorts, he is very likeable and gregarious. With his neat hair and slight build, he could pass for any other kind of businessman. Loaded with charm, Glen represents the quintessential gigolo. He loves sex. More than a livelihood for him, it's a passion. As a matter of fact, all his endeavors are sex-oriented. As a sideline, he produces x-rated videos, distributes them, finds the talent and, of course, stars in his own private porno scenes. It seemed to us that if Glen had one wish, he would want to stay in the business forever.

Toni: How did you become an escort?

Glen: I'm forty now and I've been doing this since I was twenty-nine.

A guy I used to see at a bar here in Dallas, we were talking, you know. Like most guys you tend to talk a little about sex, about what you like to do, and after a while he told me what he did — meeting women and working escort. This guy had been doing it for a couple of years. At first I thought he was just putting me on, but then he asked if I would be interested in meeting one of the women that he had met with, to kind of fill in for him, you know.

He was telling me that because he had a serious relationship going, he thought it was time to get out of the business. Chris, his name was. Couple years older than me. He was just tired of it, I guess.

It sounded exciting to me. I figured, "Sure, why not? I'm gonna get laid and get paid for it. Damn right I'll do that." So he called his friend and she said fine.

I went over there and met with her for a while and stayed for maybe an hour, and, you know, had some sex with her and left. That was my first client.

Dane: What was she like?

Glen: She was late thirties, blond, nice-looking and a nice person. I think that the type of women you get involved with as an escort tends not to be stereotypical.

Dane: What do you think are the common assumptions about a woman who uses an escort?

Glen: Oh, that she is about fifty-five, kind of dumpy looking. And that she's either a wealthy widow or a woman whose husband doesn't have time for her. Those are almost all incorrect, from what I've seen.

I found that the women tend to be just regular people. You know, some are hot-looking, some aren't, some are wealthy, some aren't, some are just regular working people.

Toni: Some are young?

Glen: Quite a few, which is not well known. You frequently find girls in their twenties and rather attractive, too.

Toni: OK. Why are some of the women, particularly the younger ones, choosing to use a male escort?

Glen: I'm actually reluctant to ask them because I think it can be embarrassing for them, but my personal feeling is that they have particularly high sexual drives. That's what I think it boils down to.

And I don't think it's the case of people saying, "Well, they want companionship." I think that's all crap. I think the woman wants sex and that's the end of it. You want companionship, get a dog. It's a lot cheaper.

Dane: Were most of the women single or married?

Glen: About half and half, whereas I think people would tend to think most are married. Another stereotype.

Dane: Do you think there are many guys working as escorts?

Glen: Sure. It's just kept a little quieter than men who use call girls.

Toni: People who are going to read this book are probably going to wonder why would a young woman, one's who's attractive, has some money, and has this high sexual need, why is she choosing to pay for it? Why couldn't she just go cruise a bar and find a man and get it for free?

Glen: I think maybe because at the time that she's paying an escort, they don't want to get involved. They don't want an entanglement. She might have just gotten through a divorce or broken up a relationship. Remember, it's just a business. When the time's up, it's over. You go your separate ways.

If she goes out and meets a guy in a bar, and they go home together and have sex for the first time, as far as I'm concerned, any guy I know, that's kind of a ticket to expect sex on every date after that. I mean, that's the way it goes. And the girl may not want that. She may just want the sex the first time. She may not want a relationship. She may not want complications, you know? Paying for an escort avoids all that. It's easy. It's clean. She's in charge.

Toni: Do you feel that women want to have control and paying for it provides that?

Glen: To some degree you're right, Toni. But sometimes there isn't any control once she's in the situation.

Dane: So a woman isn't always safe when she pays for it? What can happen?

Glen: Guys can do some crazy things. Beat up a woman, for example. Get a little too rough. There's some flaky guys working escort. Some of them actually hate women. But that could be true of a guy you pick up in a bar, too. You just never know.

I think your chances of running into a dangerous situation with an escort are minimal. You just gotta be careful. Use your head. Women are basically safe in using an escort, but it's naive to think there is absolutely no risk.

Toni: Did you run into some women that you thought really didn't like men? That they were buying this service, choosing to pay for it to make the man feel powerless? Kind of like a "You're bought, you're paid for" attitude?

Glen: Yeah, it goes back to that control thing. But usually what happens is, it's a one time deal. If she calls back, you say no.

Toni: Do you remember an incident like that?

Glen: Oh, yeah. This was a referral. The woman was about thirty-seven. We met for a few drinks at a bar. Then we went over to her apartment. It was one of those neighborhoods in Dallas that looked like people tended not to stay for years and years. Transients, you know. A place with a high turnover.

So anyway, she started getting a little bit flip. I don't remember exactly what she said, but her attitude and her demeanor were such that she, well, if it was a guy, you'd call him a wise guy, you know, a smart ass. Someone who is being condescending and rude.

Anyway, she asked if I was into bondage, and I'm really not. She wanted to be dominant but I didn't like her tone so I didn't pursue it. She got sarcastic and said stuff like, I think I'm really special because I make my living off women, and so on. Her comments led me to believe that she'd like to think she was in control of me, like she was buying a product or commodity. I guess that attitude really became evident during sex.

She was like, "Oh, not this. Don't do that. Not right there. A little higher. A little lower. To the east. More to the west." I mean, she was like a fucking traffic cop!

And you know, you hear the stories about guys jumping up and going to the bathroom right after sex? Well, that's what she did. Then she came out fully dressed, so it was pretty clear the party was over. I was dismissed, and she wanted me to get out of there.

She said, "OK, thanks. I'll let you know if I want to see you again."

Dane: And you never saw her again?

Glen: No.

Toni: How did that make you feel?

Glen: It was uncomfortable for me. For the first time in the business I really felt bought and paid for.

You know, with a relationship you can talk about what someone wants sexually, and after a few times you learn how to please them. But as an escort, you got one shot to do it right. That isn't always easy, but you try because that's what you're getting paid for.

Dane: Have you ever been married?

Glen: No. I was close to it once, many years ago.

Toni: When you were in that relationship, were you also working escort?

Glen: No. That was before. Like I said, I started this when I was twenty-nine. The relationship ended maybe a year before that, and I've since gone out with women somewhat seriously but never on a regular basis.

I don't think I could ever get married. I mean, what could it possibly offer me? I've seen a lot and I know there's too much out there for me to get tied down.

Toni: Do you tend to tell the women you date what you do for a living?

Glen: Yeah.

Dane: What's the reaction usually?

Glen: It's kind of mixed. Some people don't care, but I think they really do. They say they don't but I think they do.

Toni: Do you think some women actually found it almost appealing, that "bad boy" image?

Glen: Yeah, I think so, but they didn't let me know that. I think they felt that, but they didn't give me the satisfaction, the ego boost, of knowing that's how they felt.

Toni: With the married women who were your clients, what do you think was missing in their relationships with their husbands?

Glen: Sex. I think they just had very, very high sex drives, and maybe nothing else was missing. Maybe they just needed more sex than their husbands could give. I don't know.

Some stuff you hear, it's such bullshit. Like that the husband is always like in Mexico or South America wrapping up business deals, and there's always millions and millions of dollars, and that she's just sitting there lonely. That she's got this mansion where they have money and servants but no one to pay attention to her. I think those ideas work good in movies, but not in reality.

Dane: How would you bring up the issue of money? Would you discuss payment right away when they first called?

Glen: Yeah. During the call. It was always approached initially.

Dane: Do you charge by the hour?

Glen: Yeah. I charge three hundred dollars an hour. But it always ends up you're there more than an hour.

Dane: What's the most you ever got paid during a weekend?

Glen: A weekend? Well, I had a twenty-five hundred dollar job, like from a Saturday noon until Sunday night. It actually ended up costing her more because she then wanted another woman, so I brought in a hooker and that girl got paid too.

Toni: Is that fairly common in women's fantasies, having another woman participate?

Glen: I don't think I can count on two hands the number of times where I've talked to women who've been offended by the suggestion of a threesome with another woman.

Very rarely do they say, "Ah, ah, that's disgusting." Yet you could ask most guys about being with another guy, no guys will admit to it. And I don't think most guys are interested in it.

But women will say, "Well, I don't know. I've thought about it. I've never done it. Yeah, it might be all right." I had a few say, "No, I don't think so." But they don't say it with the vehemence that a guy would.

Toni: Could it be that the women you're with tend to be the more adventurous or experimental ones anyway because they're hiring a male escort?

Glen: Yes, but that's not just clients I'm talking about. That's any woman I've talked to, you know, in regular environments with regular normal girls that would never go to an escort.

Dane: Have you ever been confronted by a jealous husband?

Glen: No, but that's a fear. I have run into situations, though, where women have told their husband about me, and he hasn't been upset. They've said, "Geez, I told Fred I was with you, and he thought it was a good idea for me." Maybe it spiced up their lives, you know?

Toni: Have you had any problems with women becoming emotionally attached to you?

Glen: Yeah, a couple have tried to prolong things. But there are two factors which usually prevent it. One is the money. It can get very expensive for a woman to keep paying me. And two, I have the unique talent of being able to worm my way out of any situation.

Dane: Has being in the business altered your perception of marriage?

Glen: No, I don't think so. I think it's just me, not the business.

Dane: You said you got dates by referral? You never advertised?

Glen: No, because I've talked to guys who have advertised, and they get so many crank calls it drives you crazy. First you get calls from all the gay guys. Then you get calls from the women who just want to talk. I like to keep my home life private. That's why I never advertised.

Toni: What if you're with a woman and she isn't appealing to you? She doesn't turn you on?

Glen: That happens, of course, and you just try to make the best of it. I just close my eyes and think of someone that does turn me on. But, fortunately, I haven't had that problem too often. If it happened too much, I'd start thinking about going to real estate school or something.

Dane: How often do you go out on appointments?

Glen: Once or twice a week. That's all I want.

Dane: Has the price structure changed much in the last eleven years?

Glen: It's doubled. The basic law of supply and demand.

Toni: The women that are your regular clients, how often do you see them?

Glen: Usually once a month. And I would say someone is a regular if I see her once every two or three months.

Dane: How long was the longest you've seen one person?

Glen: Seven years. She's a single woman in her late forties. She doesn't seem to care about a love life. We get along good for the time she sees me.

You know I get the money, but after a while even with that, you have to drum up some enthusiasm for it. Sometimes it's just a job like any other job.

Toni: What do you think makes a successful male escort?

Glen: You have to be able to perform well sexually. Other guys will disagree with me. They'll say a sense of humor is the most important, or being a good conversationalist, or knowing how to act in a fine restaurant or something. But I think, plain and simple, these women are looking for sex. Their sexual demands come first and it stands to reason that the guy has to be good sexually.

Toni: How important do you think it is to be a good listener? Is that important?

Glen: Well, I think there's being a good listener and giving the appearance of being a good listener. I think that's more important.

Toni: What kind of advice would you have for a young guy that wants to be an escort?

Glen: Well, escorting is not a full time thing with me, even though I do real well with it. So I might suggest that a guy has an additional source of income. With me, I do very well producing videos.

And it seems every guy fashions himself a big stud; "Oh, I can do this," you know. Well, it's not that easy. You gotta be special. The right look, the right attitude. That's how you keep your clients, by being everything they want you to be. You're their fantasy.

You see, the women tend not to flip around too much. When guys go to call girls, they may go to one once or twice and then go to another and another, looking for variety. Women tend not to. They tend to have one escort and stick with him, which creates the notion of "regular customers."

Dane: What do most women like to do? What are their sexual preferences?

Glen: I would say that what most women wanted, across the board, was touching them, caressing them, leading up to a certain position. They also enjoyed a lot of oral sex. Regular missionary position and a doggie position were the favorites. Anything you could put your imagination to. Like over a couch and all that stuff.

But I think all they want is a lot of sex and they don't want to stop. Some women have wanted to get involved with dildos and toys and stuff. Well, that's fine if they have their own because I don't carry around a bag of toys.

Dane: Do you still get referrals?

Glen: My last referral was last summer. I'm very picky; I don't need this business really, so I can pick and choose.

Toni: What do you want to do when you get out of this business?

Glen: I'm already branching out. I'm doing some movies now. I've filmed and sold a couple of scenes. You know, sexual scenes, x-rated scenes that I've filmed at my house.

I've sold them successfully, not as a home movie but as what they call a "loop," where they take a section of footage and combine it with another film. I don't know if you follow the adult film business much, but they repackage them frequently just for a scene. You know, it won't be a continuous movie. It'll be a scene of some sex specialty that they'll put together.

So, I sell the scene. I get paid for it, and then one of the producers will splice it in with other scenes to make a certain movie. Say it's on blonds, or guys with big dicks, or anals or something. They tend to combine five or six scenes together and sell it that way. It's a good income and I have a lot of fun doing it.

Toni: What was your favorite encounter?

Glen: My favorite was with a Chinese girl who had a lot of money. Chinese, you know, but American, a student at the University of Texas.

And when she called me, she was kind of coy with how she got the referral. I started thinking that some guy was playing a joke on me. I mean, this girl's nineteen. What's she need an escort for?

Well, it turns out she had been speaking to another customer, this older woman I see, at some charity event. Apparently, they had some drinks together and I guess this woman let the Chinese girl know what she was doing as far as sex goes. And so that's how it came about.

Now, I was a little bit suspicious, but I picked her up anyway. I thought, "Too bad this doesn't happen all the time." Because she was young and pretty, you know, and really wild sexually! I had a great time with her.

Over the next couple of months she introduced me to another college friend of hers. She was twenty-one, and Chinese too. I thought, "Geez, this is really good." And I tried to figure a way that I could get them both together, but they didn't want to do it. And after a while, that was it.

The next year when school started, I gave them a call, but they never called back. So I said, "Well, I'm not going to make a big deal of it."

And I guess that kind of explodes the theory about them all being older, desperate and lonely, huh?

Toni: What are some of the positives about being an escort?

Glen: Some good sex and a lot of money. Let's face it. It's not a very intellectual profession. I mean, it's not like you get stimulating conversation or anything. But it's great money and it takes two, three nights a week. It doesn't take a lot of effort or intelligence on my part. You don't need a closet full of designer clothes. That tends to be movie stuff, like that movie years ago with Richard Gere where he was a gigolo and the lady was always buying him clothes and suits and cars.

It's not a profession. It's not a career. But I am a legitimate businessman. I take, they take, everybody wins.

Toni: What do you think other men think about escorts? Do you think they feel threatened? Envious?

Glen: I don't know. Maybe. I mean, you get that once in awhile. A look of envy in the eyes, an intense curiosity about it. Lots and lots of questions.

Dane: Do you think you'll be doing escort for awhile yet?

Glen: No. I'll be hitting forty pretty soon. I'm going to be retiring. I think guys in their thirties are probably at the best age to do it just because they look better than an older guy. And a woman would tend to want a young guy. I suppose that would parallel the hooker business. I mean, forty-year-old hookers, I don't know what happens to them. And who knows what happens to forty-year-old gigolos? I mean, is there a home for old gigolos out there somewhere?

Ann

The escort Ryan referred Ann. She had never hired him for his "call boy" services. They had met at a party and struck up a conversation.

We chatted over bagels and coffee in a Ft. Lauderdale cafe. Flamboyant, colorful and straight forward, she spoke frankly and enthusiastically about her sexual adventures with Michael who was her gigolo for some time. She expressed real enthusiasm, and became more and more animated as she warmed to the subject of our conversation. The shocked looks from those seated at nearby tables delighted her and spurred her on to share more and more intimate details about her experience.

A woman of the 90s, Ann seemed to be full of energy. She is slim but buxom, and has long, raven black hair.

Toni: Can you tell me about your experience hiring a male escort?

Ann: I was lecturing at the YMCA on diet and health. I remember having a full class at the Y, and I'm up there at the front talking, and way in the back of the room I see this young kid who had come in from playing basketball. He had basketball shorts, and he had this bronze body that was soaking wet with sweat. I mean, it glistened, and he was leaning up against this back wall, and he was eating a candy bar.

Toni: As you were lecturing on nutrition?

Ann: Exactly. And he had made it very obvious that he was eating a candy bar. I even know it was a Butterfinger, and he was sucking it, licking it, pushing it around his mouth. He was playing with it, and after the lecture was over he disappeared.

However, one of the girls who worked at the Y said, "You have a fan." And I said, "Who?" And she said, "Michael. Didn't you see him standing in the back of the room?" And I said, "I saw a kid standing there." And she said, "Well, he's an interesting kid. There are a lot of wealthy women in this world that pay Michael an awful lot of money for his time."

And I said, "Well, if he can eat a woman like he can eat a Butterfinger, I can understand why." And that was the end of the conversation.

Toni: So what happened next?

Ann: The next week I was back — this was a series of six lectures — he shows up again in the back of the room. And he's got a candy bar again, and we're going to go through this whole routine again. And it was almost as if he was talking to me, seducing me, without saying a word the distraction was mighty. Absolutely incredible.

The Y had a pool, so he had a white towel thrown over his shoulder and jeans thrown on that were very provocatively unbuttoned, and he was watching me.

At the time, I was forty-five, and Michael was twenty-one, so I think our ages were appropriate for what was going to happen to us. Interestingly enough, I had thought the previous week that it would be really nice to pay someone. I'd been married a few times, and I'd known a few men. And I thought that if you bought something, it belonged to you, and if it belonged to you, then you could do anything you wanted with it. I mean, if you buy a car, you can do anything you want with your car, so I thought it would be really neat to pay a man because then you could own him for the time that you had him. And he would have to do everything you told him.

And the money had to be part of it. So I was very intrigued with him.

Toni: So you're in the front lecturing, he's in the back. What happens next?

Ann: Everybody leaves. I'm packing up my things, and he's still standing back there eating his candy bar. And I feel my heart begin beating really fast because I know he's not exiting like he did the first time.

I had always had a lot of men in my life and I was considered quite an exciting woman myself, so I was very comfortable with my own sexuality. And I thought, sex for hire, so to speak, was really intriguing.

As I packed up my stuff, I passed by him and I said to him, "You're really quite a distraction." And he said, "I am." I said, "I'm up there talking about how to eat properly and good health habits, and you're out there eating a candy bar." He said, "I thought you'd never notice."

Toni: As he's provocatively unwrapping it, sucking on it, et cetera?

Ann: Exactly. So I said, "Well, you're a difficult man not to notice." And at that moment I wanted him to pursue me. So I walked past him, out to my car. And yes, he shows up at my car, and he says, "So where are you going?" I said, "I don't know. Where do you want to go?" He said, "Do you drink coffee?" I said, "Yes. Come on, I'll buy you a cup of coffee."

That was interesting because I was already into the, "I'll buy you" mode. I didn't ask him, it was just, "Get in the car, I'll buy you coffee." And my friend Myra was supposed to join me — we were meeting at a small restaurant down from the Y — and when she came in, she took one look at him, one look at me, and she said, "Well, hi, Mrs. Robinson, how are you doing?"

Toni: What was Myra's reaction to what was going on between you two?

Ann: She was extremely uncomfortable because there was such a sexual energy going between the two of us. She left.

At the end of coffee, we go back to the car, and I said, "How expensive are you?" And he said, "Oh, someone told you what I do for a living." And I said, "Yes. How expensive are you?" And he said, "How expensive do you want me to be?" And I said, "Well, I'd like you to be expensive but affordable." And he laughed and said, "It's open for negotiation."

So he said, "Are you going to be here next weekend?" And I said, "Yes." And he said, "Then maybe we can go for something more than coffee."

And I said, "Are you up for the job?" And he laughed and said, "I always have to be up for the job." So the next week, it was just understood.

I brought a couple hundred dollars with me. And that began a long and interesting relationship with Michael and myself.

And it was going to have complications because in the middle of it, I was going to move in with another man. But anyway, I like to walk on the wild side, and if I was going to pay for it, I wanted to do what I wanted to do.

Toni: How many times were you actually with him?

Ann: I would say at least ten or twelve.

Toni: And each time, it was what — two hundred dollars?

Ann: Actually, there was no set fee. I gave him what I thought he was worth.

Toni: Describe what he looked like.

Ann: 5 feet 11inches, sandy brown hair. Huge hazel green eyes. Very tan. And he had that great slim build where you could see his stomach muscles And he had great obliques, an incredible chest, tremendous vascularity. His veins were like ropes that wound through his arms and legs. Square jaw, extremely handsome.

And Michael was very sensuous. In fact, more sensuous than I had counted on because after we had our tryst, he didn't want to stop seeing me. And he wanted to waive the fee.

Toni: That's an interesting twist!

Ann: And the danger was, by that time I was living with Sean, and he was calling my home, and Sean was answering the phone, and he was hanging up. So I finally had to say to him, "This is over. You can't continue calling me."

I remember one night we couldn't go to my house because Sean was at the house, and Michael had a roommate, so we couldn't go there. So we decided to meet and we went out on the golf course, lush with rolling hills. He had injured himself and had a cast on his leg. First we tried to do it in the car, and with the cast it just didn't work. Anyway, we decided to do it on the golf course. So we took a blanket and laid it down on the ninth hole.

Toni: I guess he was trying for a hole in one?

Ann: Yes! Absolutely. We were having a ball, so to speak. It was just divine. We were in the missionary position only because of his cast. Anyway, we heard a sound, a ch–ch, ch–ch, and I'm thinking, "What the hell is that?" And all of a sudden we're hit with this spray from the golf course sprinkler system. This was like a fire hose being turned on you! I don't know what position he was in at this point, but it might have been enema time for him! He fell on top of me, and we tried to keep his cast dry. It was hilarious. We got back in the car, laughing hysterically, soaked to the skin. There was a lot of fun in this relationship.

Toni: Is that the part that you enjoyed the most? The fun?

Ann: Well, we had a lot of fun, but that wasn't what I really enjoyed. It was the ownership. I liked owning him. It was the first man I ever felt was bought for, paid for, and I liked that. And I liked to give him tests.

Toni: What kind of tests?

Ann: Like I hired him one night and we went out in public, and I decided that somehow or another, he was going to climax, and I was going to figure out how to do that. And do it in public.

One time I used a pot of lip gloss as a lubricant to massage him, while sitting at a full bar. There must have been three hundred people in the bar at the time, and I liked it. I liked to prolong it. I liked to keep him from coming as long as I could. And I would say, "You know, if you come before I tell you to, then I'm not going to pay you." And because I like to tease, I really enjoyed it!

Toni: Do you feel that your "teasing" added to the sexual excitement?

Ann: Oh, absolutely. And it was also why he wasn't willing to give me up.

Toni: Because he needed that as well?

Ann: Yeah. I think that teasing genuinely excited him.

Toni: Did anybody in the bar notice what was going on?

Ann: I don't think so. I didn't see anyone catching us. It started with touching his thigh. It wasn't totally planned out. I was thinking how to accomplish this. I didn't really want to crawl under the table somewhere and do something to him. But the idea here was there were so many people, so many chances for discovery. It was so busy.

Toni: How close were the closest people sitting to you?

Ann: Oh, standing beside us. Bartenders in front of us, people all around behind us.

Toni: And while your hand is massaging him, are you acting like nothing is going on?

Ann: Oh, absolutely. Matter of fact, while I was masturbating him, I had a conversation with the person to my left.

Toni: No!

Ann: Yes. I talked with the bartender. And then, deliberately, I'd look at him and go, "Isn't that right, Michael?" And he'd say, "Oh, that's right."

Toni: Do you remember what you were talking about?

Ann: I have absolutely no idea. But it was very, very exciting. We both had a great time that night.

Toni: Sounds like a very erotic encounter.

Ann: Yes. And I liked the power. I liked how excited he got when we did this off-the-wall kind of stuff. It was almost like this slave-master kind of thing. And I really got off on it. In fact, I liked it so much I began to be concerned about my own well-being! It was a terrific time for me though, because he had an incredible energy. I had never experienced a twenty-year age difference, either. And, oh, my God, his erections were unbelievable. Such power! And I liked how long he could go before he came. However, I did notice that his ability to hold out on climaxing got less the longer we were together.

Toni: What was it like the first time you were with him? What did you feel?

Ann: I wasn't nervous or anything. What I wanted him to do was — nothing. I didn't want him to do anything. I didn't even want him to move. The first time we did it in the apartment of a friend of mine. This friend had told me I could use his apartment while he was gone.

Toni: So after the Y, you took him back to the apartment?

Ann: Yes. I told him, "What I want you to do is just to lay there. If I kiss you, I don't want you to kiss me back. I want you to let me kiss you. I don't want you to respond. And I want you to let me touch you. I don't want you to touch me. I want to touch you.

Toni: What other sexual activities did you do?

Ann: He enjoyed anal sex, so we used to play proctologist a lot. I'd say,

"I think you need to go to the doctor." He'd say, "Oh, no, not the proctologist." I'd get out my rubber gloves, the Vaseline, and again, I'd tell him that he wasn't allowed to come. And then I would tell him when I wanted him to come. And by this time I understood his body pretty well, his responses. I liked that part. It was like leading him. I always liked that part. It was a total control issue with me.

Toni: Were you ever concerned about your safety with him? Especially the first time alone with a man in your friend's apartment?

Ann: I was never concerned about my safety. I always felt more powerful than he was. I'm smarter. He played the role for me. He did exactly as I told him to. I'm sure with other women, he played other roles. Maybe he was the dominant one. But for me, he wasn't wimpy, but he was very submissive.

Toni: In your past relationships, did you feel powerless? As if the man had all the power?

Ann: Absolutely. My second husband was a very dominant sexual partner, almost at times, frightening. I think I felt like men had always used me. And now I was using them. And I liked using this man. I even liked the fact that he had to take money.

Toni: Why?

Ann: Because it actually was a job. He had to perform to earn his money. And I liked that.

Toni: How was the money handled?

Ann: We'd talk about what he thought he was worth that night, what I thought he was worth. I'd bargain with him, negotiate. Sometimes I'd make him extra deals. I'd tell him what he could do to earn an extra twenty bucks.

Toni: The affair with this escort, did it change sex at all for you in your next relationships?

Ann: Well, I had always gotten bored easily. I'm an activity junkie. I like sex and men. I like to manipulate men, play with them, undress them, but then I get bored with it. I mean, I remember spending a lot of money on my bicycle. And I was so excited about it. And then one day I had ridden it and I was over it. I was bored with it. Even in the way I've earned my living, always needing new experiences.

Toni: As an executive in the diet and nutrition field, what kind of salary were you making?

Ann: Well, I owned the company. So I made extremely good money. About one hundred thousand dollars a year.

Toni: So paying two hundred dollars for an encounter was nothing?

Ann: Oh, absolutely nothing. We'd spend two hundred dollars on dinner. This way I got two hundred dollars worth of fabulous sex.

I think I did get a little frightened of Michael near the end when he didn't seem to want to let go. It was like, I hired you, you know, the job is over. And he continued to pursue me.

Toni: Did you feel freer to act out sexual fantasies with this man since you were paying him?

Ann: Oh, sure. I was constantly thinking of things that I could do with him. One time I took a very soft ballpoint pen and decorated his entire erection. I wrote sayings and slogans, drew arrows and flowers on the head of his penis. I was very creative! He seemed to really enjoy it because every time he showed up after that, he brought his pen with him!

Toni: (laughing) What else did you do?

Ann: We played with cock rings. He enjoyed playing doctor a lot. But you see, again, that's an authority thing. There you are with a doctor. He's the authority, you're the patient, you do what he says.

Toni: Do you know if Michael was being hired by other women while he was seeing you?

Ann: I don't know. I never asked. It was not a concern for me. What he did in his time off was up to him. It was none of my business.

Toni: What about the health issue? AIDS and other diseases?

Ann: Call it denial, stupidity, I mean, I didn't give it two thoughts at the time. I saw myself as extremely powerful, almost invincible.

Toni: Do you feel you got your money's worth?

Ann: Yes.

Toni: Did you ever feel that you might become emotionally attached to him?

Ann: Absolutely not. I was sexually attracted to him, infatuated with the roles we played. It was a sensuous time for me. But love had nothing to do with it. He loved oral sex, which was great, and we had exciting encounters. Hallways of hotels, laundry rooms, that kind of stuff.

Toni: How did you explain him when you were out on a date?

Ann: This is my friend Michael. That's what I said.

Toni: Did you ever tell your friends about Michael?

Ann: Well, Myra knew. My friends all knew I was extremely sexual. I loved men. I loved everything from intercourse to talking about intercourse. I loved going down on a man. I really relish that.

I never went to bars to meet men. I didn't want those sexual games. This man let me do whatever I wanted. Like one time I used silk scarves, tied them in knots, and used it on him rectally, so that when he would climax, I would pull the scarf out. That worked on the prostrate pretty well. I mean, I was inventive.

Toni: Were drugs ever part of the experience?

Ann: I would hate to do anything to interrupt the sublime pleasure of the drug of sex itself. Talk about a drug! Your body produces endorphins every time you make love.

Toni: Have you always been attracted to younger men?

Ann: Always. I've always been with men at least ten years younger than me. Now, Michael was twenty years younger. And I followed him with another lover, Jessie, who was nineteen.

Toni: Your friend Myra never expressed disapproval?

Ann: Oh, God no. She admired my energy, she said. And I think it gave me energy. I liked that feeling of power. Invigorating.

Toni: Would you ever do it again? Hire someone for sex?

Ann: Very possible.

Toni: If there's a woman out there who's thinking about hiring a male escort, what would you say to her?

Ann: Well, in this day and age, be careful! Use your head. I mean, today

I don't think there's a piece of ass out there worth dying for. I mean, today I insist on condoms with any man, not just an escort. Because you're sleeping with every person they've ever slept with. So, use protection. With every man.

Toni: Some people feel that it's worse for a woman to hire the services of a man than for a man to hire the services of a woman?

Ann: I'm glad you asked that. First, I think it takes an incredible man to satisfy a woman over and over and over. I don't come from that judgmental attitude. I see absolutely no difference. But then, living in a white man's reality has never been my choice. So I have to capitulate to what society thinks. But I think for myself. I think there are a lot of women out there who have a right to do this. And I say to them, go for it. Escorts are terribly exciting! You'll love it.

Toni: Do you have anything you'd like to add?

Ann: I'm thrilled to have this moment to share it, because while I shared it, I got to relive it again! You know, I'd make a great dominatrix, wouldn't I?

Toni: Save that for the next book, all right?

Ann: (laughing) OK. It was a wonderful experience. I'm glad I had it.

Toni: Do you think it helped you with other relationships?

Ann: Um... no. (laughs)

Toni: Did the man you were living with ever find out about your relationship with Michael?

Ann: No. And it's a damn good thing. You and I may understand this, and other women who've hired a man, but he would not have understood. And on that note, I think I'll go to the psychiatrist now. (laughs)

Toni: I heard his name's Michael. (laughs)

Kyle

Tommy connected us with Kyle whom we arranged to meet at the Yankee Clipper Hotel in sunny Ft. Lauderdale. For hours he mesmerized us with his stories as well as with his knowledge and experience in the business. And to him, that's all it was — just business. A money machine that never stopped.

Kyle is a tall, slim Hawaiian. His glasses give him an educated look and, indeed, this man is smart. Both articulate and streetwise, he has the charisma to charm women right out of their purses. It was hard not to like this guy. In fact, we enjoyed his stories so much, we didn't want to end the interview.

Dane: How did you become a male escort?

Kyle: Back when I was in Hawaii, I was a bodyguard for a well-known entertainer. He had Royal Hawaiian blood, and through him, I met a lot of wealthy women. I was amazed how many offers I got from these women to be their "private bodyguard" for an evening.

The main deal was I'd get three hundred bucks a night and then tips. I'd take them to dinner, dancing. I knew Hawaii pretty well, and then during the day I'd take them on tours.

Anything beyond just "friendliness" was negotiable. I was getting a taste of the good life, and I liked it. But the women would come and go, and I wanted access to more of them. So I figured the best place to hang out would be the exclusive beachfront hotels.

Toni: You started hanging around the better hotels to try to meet women?

Kyle: Yeah. I figured the best way would be to get in good with the front desk clerks at a few of the best hotels. They would turn me on to the women who were coming in. Women that were in their forties, fifties, and asking the right questions.

Dane: What are the "right questions"?

Kyle: Like, where's the action in town? Where to go to meet the right men to have a good time?

I only wanted to know about the upscale women, the wealthiest ones who could afford a man like me. These were the women who were staying in the nicer rooms, running room service tabs. The desk clerk knew the kind of money they were spending.

So then, the desk clerk would call me and apprise me of all the women staying there that week who he thought I'd want to meet. For that finder's fee, I gave him ten percent.

Usually the women would congregate around the pool. I'd go there and make my appearance. Soon I had built up a clientele, about twenty or thirty Canadian women. These women had property in both Canada and Hawaii, and whenever they were in Hawaii, which was often, the desk clerk would give me a call.

I did that maybe six months, and then, in addition to paying me, they began to take over all my bills. So I didn't have to pay a dime for anything, not rent, food, or liquor tabs. And I still had tips, of course, plus I was paid cash for sex, so I had plenty of spending money.

Toni: Were most of the women married?

Kyle: It was split half and half. Most were older Canadian women in their sixties. They had money themselves or their husbands did.

Dane: Did they want sex or companionship?

Kyle: Most of the time, companionship. I'd go out and have a few drinks with them, dance with them, let them have a good-looking young man on their arm when they're walking down the street so everybody sees what they've got.

Sex? If it was there, OK. If it wasn't, it wasn't. To me it was no big deal either way, unless they were really gross. And those were the girls who were eliminated right in the beginning, the type I wouldn't turn my German Shepard on.

Dane: Were they mostly attractive?

Kyle: Yeah. There were a few not so beautiful, but green is green. If you treated them nice, as far as they were concerned, that was all right. If you went out for four hours and they had a great time, that was often better than sex to them.

Toni: What was a typical date like?

Kyle: Well, I'd start off by picking them up at the hotel and find out what they wanted to do. Most of them were not tourists. They were people who owned property, so they had their favorite places to go. We'd sit around, have a few drinks, go to a restaurant, then maybe the theatre, a park, or a dance club, maybe just drive around. That was the usual agenda. In Hawaii on Kalakaua you could go two miles and hit seventy restaurants and bars. There was always action.

Toni: How did you keep from becoming emotionally attached?

Kyle: Never a problem. It was a job, you know. It was fun, though I wouldn't have done it if it wasn't. Most of them were nice. I had a great time. And if they were a real bitch, it was a short date. If they called again, I wouldn't see them.

I ran it like a business. The women were paying my rent, food, liquor tabs, which could run five thousand dollars a month. They gave me gifts too, trips and clothes. So in addition to cash, I'd get those kinds of things. I never had to worry about money. Man, I had it made.

You know, when they go to Hawaii, they want the local men. I guess it's part of the mystique, a muscular, dark-skinned native man. Plus, it's a taboo. That puts a little excitement in it.

Toni: Did they usually hire you for one night?

Kyle: Sometimes they'd hire me for two or three weeks. I'd just be on call the whole time. And each night, if I was supposed to go meet them, I'd go. If not, no big deal. They were paying for it anyway.

Dane: What was the worst thing about being an escort?

Kyle: If I'd get a client I didn't like, sometimes I'd just want to reach over and grab her by the throat and knock the living shit out of her! She's got money, thinks everybody in the world is her servant, and her attitude was, "I'm paying for you, you do whatever I tell you." I pretty much made it clear up front : Treat me like a man, I'll treat you like a lady, and we can do business.

Dane: Can you remember an incident in particular with that kind of woman?

Kyle: Yeah. I was with this woman, Gladys. She was 6 feet 2 inches, wearing a muu-muu. She was real pleasant at the beginning, but then at dinner when it came time to order, she ordered for us.

I was thinking, you don't even know what the hell I want. She ordered steak and lobster, which was OK, but that kind of set the tone for the rest of the night. I mean, she'd bark out orders like: "Get the bartender, I need a drink." And I'd have to do it.

Well, after about five or six orders, I finally said, "Look, I think we've got a problem. Let me cover my tab, and why don't we cut it off for tonight?"

And she said, "There's a certain way of reporting an unhappy customer, Kyle." I was just starting out, I couldn't afford the bad publicity at that time. I hadn't been in that hotel long enough to set my own rules. So I thought, "Fuck it, I'll just do it. How bad can it be?"

But it kept getting worse. When it came time to get in the taxi, she made me sit in the back by myself while she sat in front and told the driver where to drive. Just a whole bunch of shit like that all night.

Then when it came time to go home, I walked her to her suite and said, "Goodnight."

She said, "No. The night's not over. We'll have drinks in my suite."

So we went in, she went to the bathroom, came out in this fancy peignoir set, a see-through type long robe, you know, so she started making her move on me.

I went ahead and did what I was supposed to do, but it wasn't very pleasant. I think she was just one of those ogre bitches with money that thinks she can do any damn thing she wants to. A real man-hater.

And believe it or not, she wanted to see me again after that night!

Toni: You mentioned that an unattractive woman would bother you. When that did happen, what did you do?

Kyle: If you do get a woman who's unattractive, there's ways of doing it without sex. As long as they're happy when you leave, that's all that counts. But hey, you gotta remember, they're paying the food tabs, the car payments, the rent...

There were also some bombshells, beautiful ones. Sometimes they'd be sitting in a bar, and when you'd see them, you'd go after them. They were there, they wanted a good time, they wanted to get down to business.

Dane: How did you charge?

Kyle: Generally, it was a thousand bucks a night, plus expenses. And they picked up the tab for drinks, dinner, and everything else. If they wanted something really special, bondage, fetishes, (no S and M, that was too weird for me!), we'd negotiate. If things were going real good, then I would just tell her how much it would cost for me to be there until the alarm clock went off the next morning.

Toni: What time of day did most of your hotel dates start?

Kyle: In the morning. They might stretch out all day.

Dane: What about gifts?

Kyle: Those were great! One of them bought me a condo in Waikiki, but mostly it was smaller stuff, clothes, a watch or something.

Sometimes they'd buy me by the night, sometimes they'd buy me for two weeks. It was a thousand bucks a night and ten thousand for a couple weeks, plus whatever extra they wanted to give you. If they bought me for a couple of weeks, I'd sort of be on call, as I mentioned. Every time they'd beep, I'd go running to them. It's the best money I made in all my life.

I got to meet some tremendous people. At one party I met a very wealthy business woman — her boyfriend was a chump — and she sailed around the world and would buy all these antiques in the places she traveled, like China, Thailand, Spain, and Greece. Anyway, her boyfriend had a real nice body, real good looking, but the IQ of a palm tree.

The name of her yacht was the Lorelei, a luxury liner, and she'd fill it up with antiques, and then she'd bring her antiques back to Hawaii and ship them to the States. She'd get antiques a nickel on the dollar in those countries. That was the type of woman I'd meet at those parties. The kind of people that don't carry business cards. They're above that.

Anyway, that boyfriend of hers was really jealous of the time she spent with me. He sulked around, but he knew better than to interfere. He was my age, twenty-six, a decent athlete, but lazy as shit. He just traveled around the world with her, letting her pay for everything. What a chump.

The thing is, I think you can only do free lancing in any city for so long. Most free lancers don't last too long. After a while, I just convinced myself I'm not gonna do this anymore, and met a nice girl and married her. And then I met three more nice girls, and married them, too. I've been married four times.

Toni: Did you tell your wives about your past?

Kyle: When we were dating, sure. I mean, it's part of the package. I'm not ashamed of what I did. In fact, some people think it's pretty glamorous. I guess it just depends on your perception. I mean, sex for sale is sex for sale. But if I had the choice to do it again, I'd do it in a heartbeat.

Dane: Where do you think is the best area of the country to do this?

Kyle: Midwest, definitely. Kansas City, Chicago, St. Louis. The women are starving for it. They haven't seen a sophisticated, good-looking, worldly guy in so long, they're all over you. It's a great place to make a lot of money. Midwesterners are real easy. They're just lay-downs. There's really no hustle involved. When you're hooked up, they're there to have a few drinks, get you back to the room, do whatever they want to do to you, and say goodnight. I never spent an all-nighter with any of them. When it was done, it was, "See you tomorrow. Pick up your money and go."

Dane: Tell us about the sex. What kinds of things did your clients want to do?

Kyle: Sometimes they'd dress up in a little outfit, and you'd take your time with them. There'd be times you'd be in bed two, three hours before you'd ever have sex. There were games, too. They loved being chased around the room. It made them feel like they were sixteen years old. You know, you crawl all over them, and they say, "Oh, no, I can't. I can't." I'd say, "Please, baby, please." Sensuality goes beyond the body, I think. It's the look, the touch, the chemistry of the minds. I mean, it wasn't hard for me to enjoy myself!

Toni: So you really enjoyed it, felt no regrets?

Kyle: Well, what better deal? I mean, you ate good, you danced good, you drank good, then you got laid good. And it's all paid for.

Their hotel suites were always the biggest, the best. The restaurants were always the nicest, the most upscale. We had the best champagne, limousines every night. They're buying you clothes, giving you gifts. Who wouldn't like it??

Dane: What did they want sexually?

Kyle: When they were with me, they got to be whoever they wanted to be. If they wanted to be the biggest slut of the year, they could do that with me. They could be anything, do anything, short of knives and guns. Some of these ladies had filthier mouths than I did. At home they're straight-laced, business suit types, with an image to portray. So when they were with me, behind closed doors, they could be whoever they wanted.

Toni: So what actually happens behind the closed doors?

Kyle: Well, if they were really turned on in public, I knew it was going to be a good night. I'd do some pretty outrageous things, too. Like discreetly feeling a woman when we were dancing. Once, in a restaurant, I went under the table, lifted this woman's dress, tickling her thigh. She really liked that! And I'd be wondering how she'd be holding back the excitement on her face.

There's one hotel restaurant right down the beach with a pool and a bar. Sitting in the bar there's these windows where you can look up and see people swimming, but they can't see you. Sometimes they actually press their faces up to the glass and don't have any idea you're watching. That's one of the bars I take women to.

We'd get in the pool, I'd work her swimsuit off and do her right in front of the window. Later, I'd take her downstairs for a drink. We'd sit there in the bar and she'd be looking at the pool and eventually she'd catch on when she saw other people swimming, not knowing we could see them. And she'd go, "Oh my God! Did we actually do that in front of other people?"

I did that a lot, because I believe most people secretly want to be an exhibitionist. This is a way of making that fantasy come true for them.

Toni: Did the women ever feel inhibited?

Kyle: When you're paying and you're lusty, it doesn't make a whole lot of sense to be inhibited. Some of them were so nice, I would have paid them! And if their nipples were hard, you knew you were doing your job. Then you'd just keep on working your way down.

Dane: I know they were financing the date, but who actually paid? You or her?

Kyle: I paid for the date. With their money. They'd give me cash or a credit card. They paid me a thousand bucks a night, on the average. Special sexual requests were extra. And they usually tipped me a couple hundred. Plus I got a kickback from the restaurant I'd take them to. All in all, I was making at least five or six thousand dollars a week.

Toni: Did being an escort help you in your relationships with women?

Kyle: Actually I think it hurt more than it helped. Sex-wise, it helped. Because there was nothing that would surprise me. I'd do whatever she'd want. But I seem to have lost my sense of intimacy somewhat. Maybe the business did that, I don't know.

I can do a real good soap box if I want to, acting like I'm desperately in love, but I could just as easily turn and walk away, and never look back. When you're so used to going in and having sex and getting paid, and making sure there is no relationship involved, you don't know how to open up. I don't think I know what intimacy is anymore. I mean, I've seen guys in the business so long, they're emotionally dead.

Dane: What are the women like?

Kyle: One of them had a lousy family life. She couldn't stand up to her family. Her brother was in upper management, a vice president of one of the professional sports teams. She had no self-esteem, no confidence. If the brother snapped his fingers, she'd do whatever he said.

Well, the image of the team is extremely conservative and that definitely wasn't my style. After I'd had a few drinks, her brother would tell me, "You've had enough." He was that type, real uptight. She never did break away from him, but I ended up becoming friends with him. And he turned me on to a lot of other connections in the professional sports world.

With the players on the road all the time, you wouldn't believe how many bored wives are left at home, looking for someone like me. I made some of my best money servicing those women.

Toni: Have you ever felt like you were bought and paid for?

Kyle: Hey, I've been with billionaires. But when it comes down to sex, the bottom line is: Everybody's equal.

Sometimes the more money they have, the more submissive they are. They're aching to be dominated. This one lady I had, tough tycoon during the day, but at night she'd be crawling on the floor, doing anything I'd say, begging me to spank her.

Then the next day, she'd be up in her twentieth floor skyscraper office hiring and firing people, treating everyone like shit. I got the biggest kick out of that. She'd be barking out orders, having everyone cringing, throwing her weight around, and I'd march right in, shut the door, and say, "On the floor, bitch. Now." And she'd be there, on the floor, in her two thousand dollar Gucci suit. It was a pleasure doing business with her.

Dane: Tell us about some of the other women.

Kyle: Janis was around for just two weeks of hard fucking. That's all she wanted. This was in Hawaii. She was on vacation, a second grade teacher, real proper. Said she'd just gone through a bad marriage. She was there on a credit card, and she told me, "I want to do three things while I'm here: drink a lot, dance a lot, fuck a lot." And I said, "Well, hi, my name's Kyle. You got a deal."

So for about two weeks, that's all we did. By 10 a.m., we'd be on the beach. By 11 a.m., we'd be in the room. By noon, we'd be back on the beach. Then we'd do some drinking and more fucking. She never wore anything under her dress. She was always available.

She wanted to do it in a restaurant once, in the men's room. So I did her on a urinal. It was one of those places where I got my kickback, so I told the owner there, "Do me a favor. For about fifteen minutes, don't let anyone in the bathroom. So he put up a sign, "Out of Order."

Did it in a cemetery on a grave stone, too. She really got off on that. I mean, this girl got excited at the sight of a zipper.

After two weeks she gave me her address and went home. I wrote her a letter trying to find out if she was going to come back, and if she was, the next time was on me. I mean, I don't know who enjoyed it more, me or her. The letter had my return address and phone number.

Didn't hear anything for four weeks, so one night I called. A guy picked up the phone, which surprised me, and I asked if I could speak to Janis.

He said, "Who's this?"

And I said, "My name's Kyle. I'm a friend of hers."

And he said, "So you're the cocksucker who wrote that letter."

And I said, "Who the hell are you?"

And he said, "I'm her fucking husband!"

I said, "Is that right? Well you dumb motherfucker, you ain't doing a very good job then," and I hung up. I mean, he's in Pennsylvania. I'm in Hawaii. What's he gonna do?

Toni: Is Hawaii a good place for a male escort?

Kyle: Well, it was when I was there. Tell you what, though, Puerto Rico's not a good place for a male escort. Too much machismo. I got into a lot of trouble and had to leave San Juan. I was working the beaches. I had one client that wanted to be with me all the time. He was gay and it just started getting to the point where I was supposed to switch to that side of the life or something, and that just wasn't going to happen. He didn't take that well.

He had connections, and he was going to make it really difficult for me. He started cutting off my business, chunk by chunk, for me. He found out who my clients were and threatened to expose them if they continued seeing me. My clients were powerful politicians, bankers, businessmen, and I was losing them right and left.

The last couple weeks I was on the run and I had to get out of Puerto Rico. He had the airports blocked. He was watching the marinas. I mean, this guy was big. I changed my name about twenty different times, dyed my hair, put on glasses. Finally, I slipped on a plane, and he was at the gate on my heels yelling after me as we took off!

I almost didn't make it out. I'd still be doing it, if that hadn't happened. From Miami I went on to Boston and learned a little trick about getting in good with the concierge of the better hotels, like around Park Square, because that's the first person guests ask when they want to find action. He'd charge me a percentage for every woman he'd hook me up with.

Bottom line, you run it like a business, it works.

Dane: Have you had any sexual experience with people from other cultures?

Kyle: The Japanese are the most perverted people in the world. Very perverted. Their society is very structured, male-dominated. The men totally rule the women There's no room for disobedience.

One guy, his name was "Oh," he owns a lot of rooms in the Hawaiian Islands — short, little fat dude with glasses — he's worth hundreds of millions. He bought a large hotel chain, has hotels everywhere. Anyway, most of them, when they're with a woman, they'll last about fifteen seconds. Genetically, they're kind of inferior, you know? Repressed in their society so that when they hook up with a good female escort, a girl who knows her trade good, she can seduce him during dinner. Rub his legs, show cleavage, the real teasing routine. I mean, that's the easiest money they ever made. Because they get into the room, and within twenty minutes, they're done. And fifteen of that was getting undressed. The girl would shower, pick up her money, and go. She could have ten Japanese men a night and still not be tired.

When it comes to sex, they're wimps. They're totally dominated. The woman tells them what position, when, where, and why. These guys are submissive in the bedroom. Well, I can't speak for the whole race, but these are the guys I've met.

Now, Japanese women, on the other hand, are just the opposite. They're so repressed that when it comes time in the bedroom, they just can't get enough. They want to come at least ten times. You had to be extremely durable. And they're not that sexually trained, so they don't know how to get a man aroused again.

It was strange. The man, get him in the room, he's a mouse. The woman, she's a tiger. But take them out in public, and he will give the orders and she'll do what he says. It's interesting. Most of the time when you find a person who's extremely aggressive in public, they're often just the opposite in private. And when they're real cool and collected in public, in private, they can't get enough.

Dane: How does that compare with American women?

Kyle: Well, most of the women I dealt with, they just wanted to be what they couldn't be at home, and they were willing to pay for it. If they wanted to be treated like shit, that's what I'd do. "Take your fucking clothes off," I'd say. I'd make them play with themselves while I'd watch. If they wanted to be treated like a lady, I could do that, too.

Toni: Did you have a set routine sexually with the women?

Kyle: No. Each woman was unique, so I'd try to figure out what she'd like. Sometimes they'd tell me exactly or guide me along.

Toni: What about kissing? You haven't mentioned that.

Kyle: No. No kissing. I didn't like that. Didn't enjoy it. But I'd work around the ears, the necks, then I'd work on the breasts a lot. Sometimes a woman would put my hand on a certain part of her body to show me what she liked, stick it on her backside, or on her feet, or shoulders or something.

Dane: How would you break into the business today?

Kyle: I'd got to Boca and Palm Beach. Check out the good hotels. I'd look in the newspapers, community calendars, and find out where the community clubs meet. I'd meet women business owners by networking at the clubs. I'd have a set of business cards printed up, be a business consultant or whatever. I'd even work the Chamber of Commerce.

During the season, I'd find out where the tourists go, what hotels, beaches. I might even head down to Miami and work Collins Avenue. A lot of good Jewish money there. I'd check out South Beach and head on down from there. From what I know, the Jewish women are frugal with their money. I'd find the ones in their fifties or sixties. You know, where the husband's dead but they still know how to have a good time.

Another way to do it is to work the bars, the nice ones where drinks are five bucks apiece. I'd wear Bally shoes and Armani suits because that automatically catapults you into a nice money level.

I'd talk to desk clerks at the nice hotels. I'd follow the good-looking female desk clerks when they leave work and if they went to a bar, I'd go too. Then I'd get a conversation going and start dating them. After a few dates, I'd make a proposition. I'd tell them whatever I earned, we'd split, just hook me up with some good people. I'd say, "We'll make four thousand dollars in a weekend." You see, they're in the tourist business. They know what the tourist wants.

In Hawaii, in the big hotels, when the group tours come in, they're assembled in a big lobby, sometimes three or four hundred people. What you want to do is get in as a greeter. That's someone who promotes events, like luaus and shows, and tries to get the tourists to buy tickets for them. You get a kickback on each ticket sold. And it's a good way to meet women. You get to find out who's single and what they're interested in, who's in town for a good time.

Females who want to have a good time are buying nothing but night-club tickets, so you look for that. They're not going to the exotic gardens and tropical forests. You'd also have a listing of hotel rooms, and you could find out who's traveling alone or who's with a group of friends and who's paired off.

Toni: What are the differences between male and female escorts? Who makes more money?

Kyle: Females, definitely. But I don't think they have as much class. They're more crass. I mean, all a female escort has to do is lie there, For a man it takes a little more.

Dane: What do you think a good escort can make in a year?

Kyle: I think a good male escort can make six figures. Where else can you have this much fun and get paid for it?

The Sheik and the Gigolo

Early movie goers could never forget Valentino in his role as *The Sheik* of Araby. The movie reflected the public's fascination with the exoticism, opulence and mystery of the sultans and harems of the seraglio.

The twenties were the twilight years of the Ottoman Empire. Spanning portions of three continents, Asia, Africa and Europe, the Ottoman Empire collapsed following World War I ending a dynasty that had endured for more than six centuries.

There was a striking parallel between early twentieth century American and ancient Persian society — the power that women held in each.

Contrary to popular belief, the sultan's wives were not merely pampered and spoiled concubines; they enjoyed a long history of influence within their sumptuous and labyrinthine prisons. Compared to the common woman whose life was one of toil and deprivation, the sultanas enjoyed all the benefits that accrue to wives of wealthy and privileged men.

After Suleyman the Magnificent died in 1566, the ambitious palace women took advantage of a succession of mentally handicapped and juvenile sultans to gain control in the government. Mothers and wives plotted and schemed behind their veils while the apathetic sultans devoured pastries, popped opium pills and guzzled raki, an anise-flavored Turkish brandy. The women exercised great power over the court, involving in their intrigues the palace eunuchs whose job it was to attend them.

Partnership in political intrigue was not the only basis for the relationship between the sultanas and their eunuchs. Because the sultan required that they undergo castration as a condition of employment, the eunuchs enjoyed easy access to the most private chambers of the harem. Some eunuchs were quite ingenious in devising ways to please their women. The close relationship between the ladies and their eunuchs served the sultan's purpose, too, for he was freed to pursue his own pastimes. The eunuchs, of course, were no threat to the purity of the ruler's blood line.*

Mozart's opera *Abduction from the Seraglio,* a tale of palace intrigue and illicit romance produced in Vienna in 1782, recounts a pasha's difficulties preserving the fidelity of the women of the seraglio. The eighteenth-century French philosopher, Montesquieu, also treated this theme in his *Lettres Persanes.* In a letter to the sultan Usbek, Roxanne, one of his five wives, says: "Yes, I cheated you; I seduced your eunuchs, I scoffed at your jealousy, and I knew how to turn your horrible seraglio into a place of delights and pleasures."

"Seduced your eunuchs?" Yes, indeed. Some eunuchs, *sans* testicles but with penises intact, could copulate and engaged in passionate love affairs with the sultan's wives. Harem ladies prized them because they came with built-in birth control. Eunuchs who were without penises became adept at other ways of pleasing their mistresses, including petting, aphrodisiacs, sex

---

* There were other practical reasons for the practice of castration. Historical novelist Mary Renault tells the story of Alexander the Great through the eyes of his eunuch, *The Persian Boy* named in the title. Alexander, one of the greatest military minds in history, conquered all the known world three hundred years before Christ. He took a eunuch with him into battle because the rigors of war were too much for a woman.

The practice of castrating boys was commonplace in many parts of the world until the mid 1800s. During the seventeenth and eighteenth century, the most highly prized male singers in Europe were the *castrati* whose angelic boyhood voices were preserved at the expense of their manhood.

Eunuchs have been employed since remote antiquity in many cultures as guardians and servants of women. Because of their positions at the right hand of the very powerful, they became trusted confidants and could influence their royal masters. In fact, eunuchs served as political advisors in China as early as the Chou period (c. 1122-221 B.C.). In *Harem: The World Behind the Veil,* Alev Lytle Croutier writes that, because Confucian tradition included the belief that the entire body had to be buried in order for the deceased to reach heaven, Chinese eunuchs carried their pickled parts around in little jars of brine. Roman emperors Nero and Claudius also employed eunuchs to look after the women of the court.

toys, erotica and oral sex. Less inventive husbands no doubt suffered by comparison.

It is important to note that it was men who employed the practice of castration on other men in order to protect their women. What was left depended on the particular technique used to neuter the young man. In some cases, only the penis was cut off resulting in a eunuch who still retained his sex drive and could produce sperm but lacked the tool to deliver. In one method, a razor sliced off the penis and testicles in a single swoop. A tube was inserted in the urethra, the wound cauterized with boiling oil, and the castrated male then buried in a fresh dung hill and given a diet of milk. He stood a better chance of surviving the experience if he had not reached puberty.

In yet another method, the testicles were bruised, twisted or seared, destroying the capability to produce sperm. Eunuchs with either penises or testicles were not sexless.

Missing parts aside, eunuchs were in many respects the precursors of the gigolo. Some eunuchs, such as the chief black eunuch, even became quite rich. In the beginning of the twentieth century, the harem eunuch simply attended to his mistress' toilet and acted as her companion, accompanying her on sorties into the outside world.

Eunuchs died out with the passing of the Ottoman Empire and the abolishment of polygamy in 1926 by Kemal Atatürk, then President of the Turkish Republic.

Tommy

We met Tommy at a hotel on Ft. Lauderdale Beach where we had found him through the desk clerk. Apparently, he was a regular at the hotel. When we spoke to him on the phone, we told him what we looked like, a redhead and a blond wearing black leather jackets, so he couldn't miss us. We arranged to meet with him at 3 :00 p.m. By 3:30, we were still waiting and about to give up when we heard someone call, "Dane? Toni?" It was Tommy. Later, he revealed he had been watching us in the lobby for half an hour just to check us out.

At 6 feet, 1 inch and 180 pounds, twenty-four years of age with wheat-colored hair and a chiseled young body, he was both handsome and strong. But his depression and vulnerability left us with a feeling of sadness which we still remember vividly. This former escort had just seen too much, done too much and danced on the wild side a little too long.

Toni: How did you get started as an escort, Tommy?

Tommy: Me and my twin brother Tim — we're from New York — we left home. And when you're living on the streets, you do what you gotta do. Anyway, we came to Ft. Lauderdale.

This guy we met got us connected with two very powerful women. They introduced us to their friends. We were just eighteen, and it was pretty fun for awhile. The women were in their fifties, and they gave us all kinds of gifts.

Dane: How old were the women you were with?

Tommy: All ages. A few years ago I had a twenty-one-year-old. She had a fifty-year-old husband. That was on a big yacht. They had eight men prior to me in the last couple of weeks, all presents from her husband. And he was blowing close to one thousand dollars a shot! I've seen a lot of stuff. That was pretty mild.

Toni: Did you ever become emotionally involved?

Tommy: What do you mean, emotionally involved?

Toni: Well, like fall in love?

Tommy: I wouldn't put myself in that position. At least not with a client. I have had a girlfriend, though. She was in the business, too.

Dane: Tell us about some of your experiences with clients.

Tommy: You wanna hear weird? I'll tell you weird. One of my first ones was a husband and wife. What they wanted me to do was have sex with his wife and throw tennis balls at him! It was really weird, but it was five hundred bucks a pop. And at eighteen, that's a lot of money.

Dane: Were you supposed to hit him hard with the tennis balls?

Tommy: Yeah. (laughs) It was at their house. He was standing about five feet away, watching me make love with his wife. He expressly wanted to be hit in the crotch.

So I was hitting him hard while I was doing his wife. It was crazy! The whole bed was filled with tennis balls.

Toni: Did he want you to say anything while you were doing this?

Tommy: No. Nobody said a word.

Toni: What were you thinking?

Tommy: Well, growing up in New York, you really see everything, so it was a little weird, but I've seen worse.

Dane: Did the guy approach you? What did he say?

Tommy: He came up to me on the beach. He just said, "Hey, you wanna make five hundred bucks? " I said, "Yeah," and he said, "Then come on."

Toni: It sounds like these experiences have had a profound effect on you.

Tommy: Sure, I guess. I was only eighteen at the time. I was involved with a lot of couples back then, husbands wanting to watch me with their wives! One guy wanted to take pictures! Can you believe that? Pictures of me doing his wife! I'm not too keen on that. But I did it on the promise the pictures would stay there. But I never knew if they did.

Dane: Were the women good-looking?

Tommy: Most of them. Once in a while, they weren't. Then it was hard to get excited.

Toni: What were the husbands like, these men who would watch?

Tommy: Really cool. Open. They liked to party. Swingers, looking for a new thrill.

Dane: Did you free lance on your own?

Tommy: For the better part of it. I went with an escort agency for a while.

Toni: Which did you like better? And why?

Tommy: Being on my own. I made more money.

Dane: Tell us about the agencies. How does it work?

Tommy: You tell them what you're looking for.

Dane: So the escort agencies have a whole menagerie of guys to choose from?

Tommy: Yeah. You pick and choose, like a flavor of ice cream.

Dane: How did the escort service advertise?

Tommy: In the newspaper and the telephone book. With free lancing, it's mainly word of mouth. Sometimes ads in alternative newspapers. And you go to the right bar.

Toni: Did you ever have to handle a jealous husband?

Tommy: Yeah. I was naked in the house. And supposedly the husband was out of town. But he wasn't. And he came charging in the house with a shotgun. And he chased me out of the house, naked!

Toni: I guess that wasn't one of the ones that liked to watch!

Tommy: (laughs) Guess not. It was pretty scary, though.

Toni: Do you think working escort has helped you in your relationships with women?

Tommy: Yeah. Because women play a lot of games. And I see the games that women play. And I'm part of it. So a woman could probably never play a game on me.

Toni: What kinds of games do you think women play?

Tommy: Cheating, that's the big part of it. Getting what they want. Having sex and marrying a man just for money.

Dane: What are the problems in free lancing as an escort?

Tommy: Well, sometimes you become territorial over a woman. Some guy will be doing a woman and then I'll start doing her, and he'll be mad and confront me, and I'll say, "Your loss, my gain."

Toni: How often did you see the women?

Tommy: Depends on how good a time you had, and how horny they are. It can vary from twice a day to once a week. I saw one client twice a week for six months.

Toni: If a client becomes emotionally involved with you, how would you react?

Tommy: If there's a lot of money involved, I'd play it for a while. I would play on her want for me. It's a game, that's all it is. And you know, they get what they want. I get what I want. Everybody's getting what they want.

For the most part, it's very ritzy, glamorous, and very hush-hush. I've totally changed my appearance since I quit doing it. Cut my hair, for one thing.

Sex is just such a big thing now, and now that it's starting to become more open, that means people like you won't be writing books about this because it will already be out. People will accept it. It's just a matter of time, it's gonna happen.

Dane: Tell us about the sex clubs.

Tommy: Those are clubs where people are having sex on stage, and the audience watches. It's a good place to make a lot of money. These are private clubs, where you gotta know people to get in. Swinger clubs.

Dane: What kind of people attend these clubs?

Tommy: Very rich. Very powerful. And we're just the toys. That's all we are.

Toni: What actually happens inside these clubs?

Tommy: Everybody's in there having a good time. You bring your own liquor and everybody's doing everybody. You just go in there, become friends with someone. You can be naked or wear towels. It's the swinging lifestyle. These clubs have bars, some have couches, some have back rooms. They're kept very clean.

Dane: What kind of gifts have you received?

Tommy: My Mercedes. One for me and one for my brother. And a Corvette. And a Ferrari 328. Plus jewelry and clothes.

Toni: People see the life you've led as very glamorous, exciting, and full of adventure. How do you respond to that?

Tommy: It's not. It's full of hurt. There was a time I went through doing drugs because I was so stressed out. I didn't want to do it anymore, but a part of me did, so I was struggling with that, with the moral side of it.

Toni: So what made you decide to get out of it?

Tommy: I just got burnt out. When you're making a lot of money, you don't think about how you feel. You're too interested in the money.

But after a few years, you get burnt out on the everyday routine. All the partying. It gets to the point where you just don't get as excited, you know.

Dane: Sexually, you mean?

Tommy: Yeah. Sex becomes monotonous. It's a job. Just like any other job.

But sometimes it's fun, too. I've been on a lot of big yachts, cruising the Bahamas, the Turks and Caicos, the Caribbean. I mean, I've traveled all over. I never would have had that opportunity if I hadn't worked escort.

Toni: So at first it's easy to get caught up in the glamour?

Tommy: Yeah. It's a big head trip for any man, being with all these women. But after a while you grow out of it.

Now, I got better things to do. I know guys, they want to do it forever. That's pitiful. I say, if it's something you want to do to get ahead, do it. But then, grow up. Go on to something else.

Dane: Were you raised in a religious atmosphere?

Tommy: Military. My brother and I got away from that. That's why we left home.

Toni: Tommy, can you go into a little more detail about the emotional feelings you go through as an escort?

Tommy: Yeah. It's ups and downs. There's a really big feeling you get of being alone. In the middle of all the parties, all the women, you're just being everybody's rag doll. You're bought. You're paid for. They own you.

Toni: Were you ever mistreated?

Tommy: Sometimes when you go back to see somebody again and again, they get the idea that they own you because they put so much money into you. So they start trying to control your life. They want to know what you're doing, who you're with. You're their property.

Dane: Did a woman ever want to do something too bizarre even for you?

Tommy: Oh, yeah. A woman approached me and said she and her friend wanted to do me at the same time. I thought, OK, sure, and they were willing to pay a lot of money for it. Then it turned out her friend was a hermaphrodite. You know, a person with both male and female sex organs. So I said, no. And they offered me more money. I still said no.

We ended up coming to an agreement. I watched them have sex.

Toni: And they still paid you?

Tommy: Yeah. It was pretty wild, definitely a first.

Dane: What was a typical date for you?

Tommy: Say they're looking for a nice evening, dinner, theatre, then her place. And then, there are the ones who don't want to bother with dinner or theatre, and just want to get back to her place.

Toni: Is that traumatic at first? Going to a stranger's place with a stranger?

Tommy: Yeah. At least, when you first start doing it. But after a while, you keep your wits about you, and you know how to handle it.

There's always a chance, though, that something bad could happen. You're walking into her house, and she could be a psycho or something. Even dogs can be a problem.

I was in a hot tub at one lady's house, and she was in another room. I didn't even know she had a Doberman pinscher, and he ran out and threw all my clothes in the pool, took a big chunk out of one of my shoes, and then just stood there growling. He wouldn't let me out.

Dane: What did you do?

Tommy: I yelled, "Hey, get your attack dog out of here!" And she heard and called him, but he just stood there. I finally got out, and he followed us into her bedroom.

Toni: Then what happened?

Tommy: We started having sex and he came up and started licking me on the butt!

Dane: What was your most romantic date?

Tommy: That's easy. One time a limo came and got me and we went to Pier 66 in Ft. Lauderdale. It's a restaurant way up in the sky. It's in a tower that spins around slowly while you dine. It makes one complete rotation in an hour, and from up there you can go out on a deck and watch the city lights as you spin around.

We ate dinner, rode around in her limo, walked on the beach. And we never even had sex. All she wanted was companionship.

Toni: Did you find that many of the women were lonely?

Tommy: Yes. Most of them felt neglected by their husbands. They just wanted to feel loved.

Toni: Did you find yourself turning into a counselor for them? I mean, would they tell you about their lives, their husbands?

Tommy: Yeah. Most of them were married to businessmen who were away too much or who drank. Sometimes the husband had another woman himself.

It seems the typical woman can't give up the financial security, even though she's in an unhappy situation. So she sees other men for the love she wants.

Sometimes you don't look at it as being an escort, but as being the only person who'll listen to her.

Dane: Some of these women are a lot older than you. Not all are attractive. What do you think about while you're with them?

Tommy: I think of something erotic. Something that will turn me on. Movies I've seen or something.

Dane: What if that doesn't work?

Tommy: There's been times I haven't been able to get excited. No matter how much I would try, it was not going to happen. Then I'd say, "Look, I'm really sorry. It has nothing to do with you." And we'd find something else to do in bed.

Toni: She wouldn't feel hurt?

Tommy: Oh, no. I'd make up for it in another way, make sure she felt OK.

Toni: Have you ever been with someone very influential? Show business or politics, for example?

Tommy: Yeah. I've had a Florida congressman's wife before. I wasn't the first. And I'm sure I won't be the last. That was something she did regularly. It was through her that I got into the sex clubs.

Toni: Wasn't she afraid she'd be found out?

Tommy: No. She was too powerful.

Dane: You could have blackmailed her.

Tommy: I thought about doing it. But she was already hip to it because she was doing it with so many escorts. She already had all her bases covered. I knew it, and that's why I didn't do it.

Toni: What do you mean, she "had all her bases covered?"

Tommy: She would introduce me to influential people. Then she'd say, "These are my very good friends. And if anything ever happened, they would take care of it."

I understood what she was saying. She wasn't afraid of blackmail, she was too powerful. She would just have you taken care of.

Dane: How does a woman usually end the relationship? A sendoff gift?

Tommy: She just stops calling. No explanation. It's cold, a complete cutoff. You might see them again in the same circles, but they won't speak to you. They won't even say hello.

Dane: Where did some of these wealthy women take you on dates?

Tommy: Orchestras, operas. I've even been to private school to see one client's child in a play.

Toni: What kind of advice do you have for a guy who wants to become an escort?

Tommy: Hit the newspapers, phone books, escort agencies.

Dane: What makes a good escort?

Tommy: You gotta be smooth on your feet. Know what older women want. Some want sex, so you got to know how to get them in the mood without actually touching them. You say certain little things. You make gestures. You smooth your way into it. Make them feel special. A good thing to do is to help them make their fantasies happen. For example, if they've always wanted to role play, you make it happen. And if she just wants to talk, you pretend to be interested in what she has to say.

Dane: Is there a standard rate in the business?

Tommy: No. The richer ones will pay more. But the ones I was with, they were all rich. It was just a matter of degree. Like, if you get a real wild one, she'll shell out whatever you want.

Toni: Do agencies worry about escorts that work for them going off on their own?

Tommy: Agencies don't allow you to take customers. If they find out you do, they'll fire you. I've been fired before. But you can do it. After you're with a client a number of times, you come to an understanding that this is not to get back to the agency. You meet on the sly. And of course, she still can't stop calling the agency once in awhile or they'd get suspicious.

Dane: How do escort agencies find out if you're meeting someone on your own?

Tommy: Sometimes they'll have a driver follow you. Or they'll try to trap you over the phone, listen in on your calls. Sometimes she'll slip up and say the wrong thing, like, "Well, since we're not going through the agency anymore, maybe you can cut the price a little bit." And they'll be listening in, and you're busted. Then they fire you, and try to blackball you from other escort agencies.

Toni: Is it hard to break into the South Florida scene?

Tommy: Not Miami or Ft. Lauderdale. But Boca and Palm Beach, that's hush-hush. They don't want no one knowing. No one will talk about it out there, not the escorts, certainly not the clients.

Dane: Can you tell us a little more about the agencies?

Tommy: If you knew the background, it's a real shitty business. My girlfriend and I worked for the same boss for a while. He wouldn't work her, told her people weren't calling for her, so she wouldn't have any money, so she'd have to crawl to him. He was trying to manipulate my girlfriend into leaving me so he could have her for himself. Then he wouldn't work me, so neither of us had any money. Finally, we both switched to another agency.

Toni: Are most agencies run by men?

Tommy: No. Most are run by women. And most of the people who own these agencies are people who have been in it. People like me. Some of these women are real bitches, real cold. They tell you, you're going to do this or that with a client or you're out of here. And I've had to do it.

Dane: What about the clients who are psychos?

Tommy: Every escort eventually gets a weirdo. There are some weird, psychologically disturbed women out there.

I did a lady, and from the start, I knew she was weird, but I didn't know how weird!

The service sent me out there. She acted a little strange, like she'd mumble under her breath and stuff. She had knives she was playing around with, kitchen knives, and that made me real nervous. She'd point them at me and stuff.

She kept wanting me to stay another hour, another hour, until I'd been there four hours. She said she wanted to see me again. Anyway, I was just glad to get out of there.

Well, she found out where I lived. I don't know how, maybe she followed me home that night. Anyway, she started coming over to my house looking for me. Like, she'd be banging on the door even if I had company over. I never let her in, just tried to laugh it off at first.

Then I tried telling her to leave me alone. Then I ignored her. If I didn't answer the door she'd bang on it for like half an hour before she'd give up.

Sometimes she'd be watching my house from her car. And sometimes we'd hear strange things outside our bedroom window, like she was listening out there or something. That really unnerved my girlfriend.

When this woman called the agency and tried to book me again, I told them I wanted nothing to do with her. I thought maybe things would quiet down.

Then one night I was having a party, and she just walked right in. She marched up to me and started screaming, spitting in my face right there in front of everyone! She told me she loved me, why was I hurting her like this, and that kind of stuff. My friends were like, "Who the fuck is this?" I thought about calling the police, but when you work escort, you don't want to deal with the cops. Finally she calmed down and I got her out of there.

The next night she was waiting outside the house and she caught my girlfriend coming home, and she grabbed her and told her she was going to kill her if she didn't get out of my life. Luckily, I was home right after my girlfriend and got rid of this woman again.

But we got real paranoid after that, couldn't sleep at nights. We were always watching, waiting. I mean, this chick was psycho! Eventually it got to be too much, and we ended up moving.

I was with her just four hours, just that one night. But I mean, who knows? She could have tied me up and killed me.

Toni: Do the police turn a blind eye to the escort business?

Tommy: Sometimes they're the ones doing it! In Ft. Lauderdale, they're very, very crooked. I mean, there was this one official — he's not on the force anymore, but he corrupted this whole town! He'd go out, he made his own entrapment law, you see, where he could go out and sell you coke, and then turn around and arrest you for buying it! And then, he made a law, if you were selling fake coke, he could arrest you, too. He hauled people in for selling baby powder. He's a really bad dude.

I remember seeing this one female escort getting beat by four police officers. They ripped her shirt off, beat her head in the ground, left her crying and bruised and bloody.

One of the ladies who ran an escort agency that I worked for, she got smart. She had a very large portion of police protecting her. How did she do it? She gave them escorts for free, girls and guys, and so they turned a blind eye to her agency. That was her protection.

Toni: Do agency owners ever pay a fee to the police in exchange for protection?

Tommy: Oh, yeah. The police are in it, man. If they can make money on the side, sure, they'll turn their heads. I've seen it over and over.

Sometimes you begin to wonder. Just who are the good guys and who are the bad guys?

Dane: Do you think you'll ever get back in the business? Or have you had enough?

Tommy: I feel it's time to move on before it's too late. I see some of these guys in their late thirties still doing it, and I don't want that to be me. I got other things I want to do.

Toni: This is your chance to tell the public anything you'd like about this world. Tommy, is there anything you'd like to say?

Tommy: Just that I want them to know we're providing a service just like any other service. You can turn a blind eye, you can harass us. Still, people will continue to use escorts. So I think it should be legal.

Quasi-Gigolos — *The Fortune Hunters*

The two world wars and the revolutions which later occurred in Eastern and Central Europe destroyed countries and devastated family fortunes. Many of the oldest lines of aristocrats found themselves destitute with little left but the clothes on their backs and their fancy titles. On the other side of the ocean, America was undergoing tremendous economic growth. It was the time of the rugged individualist when taxes did not swallow a lion's share of profits, when staggering personal fortunes were amassed in every field — oil, railroads, paper, publishing, manufacturing, and retailing.

From the twenties through the early fifties, as American men earned great fortunes, American women benefited. When powerful tycoons divorced or died, their fat bank accounts, bursting stock portfolios, magnificent mansions, gleaming luxury cars, sleek yachts, and stables full of polo ponies passed into the hands of women — their ex-wives, widows and, of course, daughters.

In Europe there was class without money, in America, money without class. God makes them and they find each other, goes the Spanish proverb. What does a multimillionaire's daughter need that daddy can't give her? Why, a title, of course — princess or at least countess, duchess, marquise or baroness. American ladies of the time, bred in democracy, went gaga over titles. Acquiring an aristocratic husband fit their fantasies of marrying Prince Charming.

Of all the imported Lotharios, the three Mdivani brothers, Serge, Alexis and David stood out. The Mdivanis, erstwhile common laborers from a modestly distinguished Russian military family, arrived with an abundance of polished looks, smarmy charm and fabricated royal lineage. So successful were they at bagging wealthy American wives that they became known as the "marrying Mdivanis."

"Prince" David, the first of the Mdivani brothers to walk up the aisle, married Mae Murray, a popular starlet of the twenties. The next "Princess" Mdivani was another Hollywood heart throb, the fabulously wealthy Pola

Negri who, it was rumored, ended an affair with Valentino to marry David's older brother, Serge. Both marriages were brief, just long enough for the husbands to squander plenty of their wives' fortunes and accumulate substantial wealth of their own.

The third brother, Alec, married a debutante in Newport in 1931, but this alliance, too, quickly ended when he spotted a wealthier mark — Barbara Hutton, heiress to the Woolworth fortune. As this marriage too foundered, Hutton remarked that her money "did something" to Alec and that he threw it around "like confetti." Alec died on a Spanish highway when his Rolls Royce crashed as he was taxiing his next conquest, a baroness, to catch a train to Paris. Brother Serge died the following year from a kick to the head by a polo pony.

As adept as the Mdvanis brothers were at marrying wealth, none of the fortune hunters of the day could approach the conquests of the most famous of the breed, Porfirio Rubirosa. In his lifetime, "Rubi" managed to marry four prizes: Flor Trujillo (daughter of the filthy rich Santo Dominican dictator, Rafael Trujillo), Danielle Darrieux, (the highest paid and most beautiful movie star in France), Doris Duke (the tobacco heiress), and Barbara Hutton (formerly Princess Mdvani.)

Rubi's enthusiasm and capacity for bedding ladies was so tireless that friends nicknamed him "Ever Ready." In her revealing account of the exploits and achievements of the fortune hunters, *The Million Dollar Studs*, Alice-Leone Moats quotes one of Rubirosa's friends as saying, "He'd screw anything that moved."

Rubi's marriage to Flor Trujillo lasted five years. Even after the marriage ended, the dictator continued to favor his former son-in-law with distinguished political appointments. His marriage to actress Danielle Darieux also lasted just five years. As part of the divorce settlement, she gave Rubi their Paris home and a handsome alimony providing he did not remarry, a pact he obviously did not keep.

In 1947 when he split from Doris Duke (wife number three) after only thirteen months he kept a Paris house and a plane. Even after the divorce, she continued to carry a torch for him and went on supplying him with cash from her four million dollar annual income. Friends said that Doris and Rubi continued to have sexual relations long after the divorce.

When Rubi met Barbara Hutton, the Woolworth heiress was in the process of divorcing her fourth husband and Rubi was embroiled in an off-again-on-again love affair with one of the great beauties of the day, Zsa Zsa Gabor. His marriage to Hutton survived a mere seventy-three days but during that time Rubi accumulated nearly a million dollars in gifts and another three million at the divorce.

The tabloid and society rags of the day were enthralled by the titled fortune hunters and lavished gallons of ink on them. Rubi's reputation as an international playboy and the fact that his contemporaries referred to him as a gigolo did not seem to bother him at all. Moats reports that when he took out his guitar at night, he often played a popular song of the day, "Just A Gigolo."

Notorious for his escapades with beautiful and rich women, his airplane and fast cars, and his prowess on the polo field, Rubi was rumored to be a star player at sex orgies where the champagne flowed until dawn. Manouche, one of Rubi's many lovers and owner of a Paris restaurant he often frequented, observed that "Monsieur Toujours Prêt" would jump on anything late at night when he was drunk. She recounted an incident when Rubi knocked off one of her dishwashers in a booth at the restaurant, in front of the waiters. The lady in question, according to Manouche, was a "real monster — hunchbacked, bowlegged, cross-eyed, with a hairy mole. In short, hideous."

Speculation on the size and staying power of Rubi's physical endowment became a popular topic of conversation. In his honor, waiters referred to tall pepper mills as "Rubirosas."

Manouche reported to Moats that "it was long and pointed and it hurt" because it hit her uterus and she went on to say that he could take on two or three women in a night. She added that "it was never hard and never soft." Moats speculates that this might indicate a case of "retarded ejaculation...or...a form of priapism." (Priapism is a medical condition in which the penis remains in a more or less continuous state of erection.) Manouche opined that this condition was "the secret of his charm."

In 1965, like Alec Mdvani, Rubi died at the wheel of a fast car (a silver Ferrari convertible). Still going strong at age fifty-four, he was speeding home after making the rounds of the nightspots to celebrate a polo victory. At his funeral were many of the luminaries of the time — movie stars, politicians, aristocrats, scores of his female conquests, international jet-setters, and, incidentally, Patricia Lawford and Jean Smith, sisters of the late president Kennedy who had been assassinated just two years earlier. A friend of Doris Duke, quoted in *Vanity Fair* nearly thirty years later (March 1994), remembered Rubirosa as "the greatest gigolo of all time."

Like the passing of Valentino, Rubirosa's death marked another milestone in relations between women and their money and the men who wooed them. Although he and his cohorts were often referred to as gigolos, they did not fit Edna Ferber's definition. The fortune hunters differed from their tangoing predecessors in that they possessed something beyond diversion that women wanted: their titles. But a woman had to "make an honest man" of her playmate in order to become a countess or duchess. Ferber, as you recall, defined a gigolo as "a man who lives off women's money." Of course, the fortune hunter did not live off the woman's money because, with marriage, her money became his. Despite their wealth, in wedding instead of just bedding, women of the post-tango era got from men what they wanted, but not exactly on their own terms.

Over time the public ceased to be awed by fancy monikers, and impoverished noblemen discovered that they could, with little shame, go into business, become entrepreneurs, or exploit the boom in the tourist industry by opening their castles to the public. With the passing of Rubirosa, the last straggling roué, the romantic gigolo figure disappeared from the headlines and the American consciousness, not to return. Even Hollywood, the stomping ground of so many opportunistic ladies' men, showed little interest in resurrecting him. In relation to the number of cops-and-crooks movies released since that time, two movies, American Gigolo and Midnight Cowboy can be seen as insignificant anomalies.

Eric

In the Hyatt Hotel coffee shop on Sunset Boulevard, we talked with Eric who had answered our ad in an alternative newspaper. (We were surprised at the number of responses we received in L.A. and chose to interview Eric because there was something special about him.) Although not as articulate or educated as most of our interviewees, he was among those we liked best. He had a little-boy charm, and, strangely enough, seemed to retain an innocence about the business. He is very good-looking, tall and dark, and looks more like twenty-two than thirty-two years old.

A few weeks after the interview, we spoke with Eric on the telephone just to touch base. He was making plans for his immediate future, preparing to enter the film business, starring in locally produced x-rated videos.

Toni: How old were you when you started in the escort business?

Eric: About thirty. I'm thirty-two right now.

Dane: There seems to be a big market for it here in L.A.

Eric: Yeah, big is too small a word.

Toni: How did you get your clients?

Eric: I put an ad in the paper. It said how tall I am, my weight, that I'm experienced, discreet, and my phone number and pager.

Dane: Did you get a good response?

Eric: Yeah.

Toni: Where did you come from originally and what brought you to L.A.?

Eric: Originally I came from Santa Fe. A friend of mine who lived in L.A.was into the film business and thought I might like to try it, so I did.

Dane: X-rated videos?

Eric: Yeah.

Toni: Were you in a lot of those?

Eric: I did it only the one time, but came out here originally for that.

Toni: Do you like L.A.?

Eric: No, not really. Because I've had my whole life in Santa Fe. This is a different world. I hate the phoniness, the movie crap.

Toni: So let's start off with how you got into the escort business.

Eric: A friend of mine suggested I try it. I didn't think I was exceptionally good-looking, you know, like a handsome dude, but as I found out later, the looks, while important, aren't everything.

Anyway, this friend says, "Do it. You're well-hung." She said it could be something I might want to look into and she told me about someone in Studio City that I could contact.

So I made an appointment with this dude who had an agency. I had four appointments a week in the beginning. They wanted me to see guys, too, but I told them no way.

Toni: So someone else set the appointments for you?

Eric: Yeah.

Toni: What was the percentage then?

Eric: Half and half. Two hundred dollars for me, two hundred dollars for them.

Toni: And they would pay for the ads?

Eric: Yeah. And they gave me a beeper to get hold of me.

Toni: What was it like the first time that you did it?

Eric: It was a little weird. I was nervous about the situation. I knew the lady was married, too.

Dane: You felt weird about that, that she was married?

Eric: Yeah. But after about a half hour, it was all right. She told me, "There's nothing to worry about, you know."

Toni: Did it start out as a date? Did you take her somewhere?

Eric: No. I went right to her house and did her there.

Toni: And her husband was gone?

Eric: Yeah.

Dane: What did she say about her husband?

Eric: He was a business guy. The woman was probably fifty years old.

Dane: Was she all right-looking?

Eric: Yeah.

Toni: Had she used escorts before?

Eric: I didn't even ask her.

Toni: But she seemed comfortable with having an escort there?

Eric: Yeah. She was real cool and calm.

Toni: So then you started talking with her, getting to know her?

Eric: Yeah. The agency told me she was a regular customer, so I'm sure she's seen other guys, now that I think of it.

Toni: And she was paying by the hour?

Eric: Yeah.

Toni: So there's probably not that much time for talking when you're paying by the hour.

Eric: True. I'd say ten, fifteen minutes total.

Toni: That first time, what was going through your mind?

Eric: I was like happy I was getting paid to have a good time.

Toni: Was it scary at all?

Eric: I was a little scared, too, yeah. Because I knew she had a husband and stuff. But because I wanted to do it, I like sex, I just went for it.

Toni: Is that why you got into the business, because you like sex so much?

Eric: Yeah. Yeah, I like sex, but I also like money.

Dane: What do you think makes a good male escort? Obviously they should enjoy sex, but what else?

Eric: Listen to the lady, whatever she says, and try to make her happy and comfortable.

Toni: Did you find that the women were generally lonely?

Eric: I think so.

Toni: And they needed a listener?

Eric: Yeah, someone to talk to. They had no attention, a lot of those ladies. They said they felt neglected, their husbands were away a lot.

Toni: Do you think that is as important to them as the sexual part of it, just to have somebody to listen to them and talk to them?

Eric: About half and half, yeah. They were lonely, you know, all of them. Their husbands were golfing somewhere all day Saturday or some bullshit, and they were never around.

Their lives were a disaster so they were usually very lusty.

Dane: You were in this for a couple of years?

Eric: A year and a half.

Toni: Why did you quit?

Eric: I was getting too used to it. At the end I was seeing about twelve people a week, plus two couples. I was making a good amount of money, living a little high life style. So I said I'd better put some of the money away because this won't last forever.

Toni: When you say that you were seeing couples, does that mean the husband would be there in the room?

Eric: Yeah.

Toni: Participating?

Eric: No, he didn't participate. Only watch, they could only watch, that's it. Because I don't do men.

Toni: What was that like, to have a man watch you with his wife?

Eric: The first time was a little strange because it was the first time I ever did it with a guy watching, husband or not. But it was OK after awhile. I kind of liked it. They apparently had done that before.

Toni: You mean the husband had watched someone with his wife before?

Eric: Yeah.

Dane: Did you ever find yourself getting emotionally involved with any of these women?

Eric: I felt it could happen. But the women said it was strictly for business. You don't see them unless it's for work.

Toni: Did they ever want you to stay past the hour, into the morning?

Eric: Yeah. Some would want you to stay for as long as you would want to.

Dane: What did you charge to spend the night?

Eric: Up to fourteen hundred dollars.

Toni: Of that, did you split it fifty-fifty with the agency?

Eric: I took about 60 percent of anything over an hour. The first hour was split fifty-fifty with the agency.

Toni: Did you ever feel bought and paid for?

Eric: No. Because I knew anytime I felt like it I could just walk out and go back home. I wasn't planning on staying in L.A. forever.

Dane: Were you ever concerned about the police?

Eric: No. I just didn't want my family ever finding out what I did. And, the video, that's another thing I was leery about.

Dane: Because you were on film?

Eric: Yeah.

Toni: Tell us about the video.

Eric: It was forty minutes long. And it was with a girl that was average-looking. And basically it took me a little time to get warmed up. It was hard in the beginning because the guy had a home video camera. That's how he did it.

It was just him, me, a girl and another guy. And basically it was from start to finish. She slowly undressed me. I slowly undressed her. A little foreplay, a couple times sex. And that was it for forty minutes. They paid me nine hundred dollars.

Dane: Did she get nine hundred dollars too?

Eric: Yeah. But there was another film I was going to do for like twenty-five hundred dollars, but I didn't do it.

Dane: How come?

Eric: I don't think it's enough money. It wasn't worth it.

Toni: I'm curious about the women who were your clients. They were paying for you. Can you describe them a little? Were most of them a little older, say in their fifties?

Eric: Yeah. I didn't see any ladies under thirty other than some heavy ladies, overweight ones.

Toni: Did that turn you off, the overweight ladies?

Eric: I try to mentally psyche it out, you know.

Toni: So what do you do?

Eric: I concentrate on making them happy.

Toni: That's not what I mean. You're in a situation and you're with this woman. She's not really appealing to you. How do you get excited about her?

Eric: But that's what I mean. I just hope I'm appealing to her. And I hope I can turn her on and make her happy.

Dane: But to get yourself going, do you think about someone else or a movie star or something if she doesn't turn you on?

Eric: I can usually get turned on after a while.

Toni: How many different women do you think you've been with?

Eric: Total, I'd say about forty. That's in a little over a year.

Toni: Were some of those repeat customers?

Eric: Yeah. About four couples and I'd say about thirty-five women. But the women would see me repeatedly.

Toni: The ones that you were involved with on a repeated basis, how often would you see them? Once a week?

Eric: About every two weeks. Some three times a month.

Toni: What about the couples? The same type of thing?

Eric: Not as much. Because I wasn't really that comfortable with it. The total with the couples was probably about ten times.

Toni: Did the husband ever say anything while you were doing this? I mean, here you are with his wife. He just sat there quietly, or what?

Eric: Yeah. One guy wanted to videotape it. I said, "No way."

And I was afraid that there might be hidden cameras. That was another thing I worried about.

Eric: Yeah. I mean there's no way you would know.

Toni: Were the women you were with pretty upscale? Wealthy?

Eric: Not real wealthy, but comfortable, certainly. Probably they stayed at home most of their life. Many of these ladies weren't professional business women. Mostly homemakers and women who were divorced. They figure an escort is somebody that's guaranteed to be there for a certain length of time, and they could end it whenever they wanted. There's not a problem. When you pick someone up in a bar, you don't know what you're getting, but if you're paying for someone, you pretty much know everything will be all right.

Toni: Were drugs a part of the business?

Eric: Well, the only drug I do is smoke grass. It's not like it's a habit that you need two thousand dollars a week.

Toni: Well, did any of the women say, for example, "OK, let's start our date. Let's do some coke."

Eric: There were women that offered me stuff – drugs, drinks – but I'd just say, "If you want to smoke a joint, I'll do that, but nothing else."

Toni: Did the women really get into the fact that you were a lot younger than they were? Do you think that was pretty exciting for them?

Eric: I think that's what they wanted. Because I look real young. I'm thirty-three now, though you'd never guess.

Dane: Did you ever have a scary incident with a woman? A situation where you thought you might be in danger?

Eric: No. But some ladies have cried.

Toni: Why did they cry?

Eric: I don't know. It happened after we had done it. They weren't unhappy with me, though. I didn't make them cry or anything. I don't know, they didn't say. But they did cry.

Toni: Maybe they were unhappy with their lives?

Eric: Maybe they felt guilty or something.

Dane: Do you think they were having second thoughts or something?

Eric: Yeah, maybe.

Dane: What did you do while they were crying? Did you just let them cry?

Eric: Yeah. I'd just be real gentle with them and let them.

Toni: What did most of the women want sexually? Traditional sex or something a little more wild?

Eric: A lot of different things. One lady liked to use a dildo while I was there. She was a little on the heavy side. She used to like that for a while, you know, to have a stranger watch her pleasure herself.

Toni: Did they want to role play?

Eric: Fantasies. Some ladies wanted two guys. But I never participated in it with anybody. But they used to say that was something they wanted, two men at once.

Dane: Was there a lot of kissing and tenderness? Or just sex?

Eric: I consider kissing and tenderness a part of sex. It's part of the whole package. And most of the ladies were attractive enough, so I didn't mind kissing them.

Dane: The women who hired you, they were average to attractive?

Eric: Yeah. Just a few were overweight.

Dane: Did that ever bother you, overweight women?

Eric: No, because, you know, for the money, that's what it's all about. The money.

Toni: You looked at it as just business? You know, this is just business.

Eric: Yeah. But I could always let myself go because I'm attracted to older women and all my clients were older than me. When I was in my twenties, I wanted women in their forties. Yeah, forty at least.

Dane: Have you ever had a serious relationship?

Eric: Yeah. Eight years I went out with someone. When I was twenty to twenty-eight. Before I did escort.

Dane: Do you still think about her?

Eric: Yeah. My business broke it up. I still miss her.

Toni: Do you think being an escort has had some positive affects on your ability to have a relationship the next time you get involved?

Eric: Yes, I think so. I know that communication is important. And you need to spend a lot of time with her. And if she's got something to tell you, you listen.

Toni: A lot of men would feel that you're living the ultimate male fantasy, being with all these married women.

Eric: That's true.

Toni: And you're having a great time and getting paid for it. Is that what it's really like?

Eric: No, I don't think so. If you got someone that you haven't seen yet, the first time going there, it's a weird feeling to me because I don't know what I'm getting into.

Dane: As far as what?

Eric: The people. You talk to them on the phone for about five minutes. Five minutes, you don't know what to expect. You don't know what the lady looks like, acts like, or where the knives are hidden.

Toni: What's your opinion of a woman who would cheat on her husband?

Eric: I don't know. I think they probably don't do it until it's near the end of the marriage. At that point, it's probably beyond saving their marriage, so I don't say it's bad. I don't disagree with what they do because men do it.

Dane: How long do you think an escort can do this kind of work?

Eric: I don't know. I knew I couldn't get too used to it for too long.

Dane: Because you didn't think it would last?

Eric: Right.

Toni: Why?

Eric: Because you get older. And there's always a new guy, a younger guy coming up to take your place. So you just get out of the way.

Dane: Is there any one kinky thing that a woman wanted?

Eric: I think the kinkiest lady was the one with the dildo. She wanted to take pinches on her rear. She wanted me to whip her, slap her butt, spank her.

Toni: And did you do it?

Eric: Yeah.

Toni: How did you feel?

Eric: Weird. I said, "How hard do you want me to spank you?"

Toni: Was it kind of a game to you?

Eric: I guess. And I was wondering what she got from it. You know, how it turned her on. Because it don't turn me on, but a lot of people, it does.

Toni: What do you think was the worst thing about being an escort?

Eric: The part I hated was if the lady was married. I thought about how the husband would feel if he knew. It's a bad feeling to have, you know.

But then I also felt, like, aroused and excited because I was the one that they were cheating with. That was something. It felt really wild. I'm the one in the middle.

Dane: How often were you with long-term customers?

Eric: Five or six visits.

Toni: If you saw a woman over a period of months, and then it ended, how would it end? Would they just stop calling?

Eric: Yeah, they'd stop calling. Or they'd call for somebody else and they'd call next time for me. Maybe they just wanted variety. And the service had pictures they could look at so they always had choices.

Dane: So when the woman walks into the escort service, she can look at pictures of all the guys?

Eric: Yeah. They have shots of every escort. At least the agency I was at.

Toni: In an agency, is there ever an escort that is just an escort? I mean, say a woman hires a man to escort her to a function. Is that ever all he does? No sex?

Eric: No, I never did that. But I know a few guys who said they had. They went to some pretty good events.

Dane: You're saying there is a market for women who just want a guy to be with, without the sex?

Eric: Right. One guy went to a wedding with a lady and she paid eight hundred dollars. And he said she was all right looking, too. He had a great time.

Toni: You said they often wanted you to just listen to them. Was that ever draining for you? To listen to their problems?

Eric: Sometimes I'd pretend I was listening to them, and I actually wasn't. I didn't want to get too into their problems. And the ones that seemed the most unhappy, the ones that cried, I thought, you got to be careful with these people. Don't say nothing. You try to be nice, hug them, you know. But don't care too much.

Toni: If you had a younger brother and he said, "I want to be an escort," what would you tell him?

Eric: I'd say, "Why?" You know, "Why would you want to do that? It's not always a good thing." So I'd tell my brother, " I'd rather not see you do it. Because it's not always safe. You don't know the people." I mean, I don't know if I ever got videotaped when I was with any of these ladies, for example.

Toni: So you would tell him, "Don't do it," yet you're thinking of getting back into it?

Eric: Yeah. It's what I know.

Dane: What about the health factor? Was that a concern to you or the women?

Eric: Definitely. I used a condom. Always. Except for oral.

Dane: Did anyone put up an argument about using condoms?

Eric: Maybe one or two, but most didn't care one way or the other. They say, "It's up to you," but they would rather not. They told me they'd rather feel the whole thing, do it natural. But I'd say, "I'm going to use it."

I had my own. I used those ones that are in the blue container, with Xs on it. They're like twenty-five dollars a dozen.

Dane: What are they made of?

Eric: A sheep membrane or something. They're natural materials. Thin, but they work.

[The Center for Disease Control recommends the use of *latex* condoms in preventing the transmission of sexually transmitted diseases including the HIV virus.]

Toni: Do you think doing this helped you to assess people quicker? Could you size up a woman immediately and calculate the best thing to say to her? The best approach to use?

Eric: Well, sure, to some extent. I mean, I always used to say nice things to them, like: "You look beautiful. How are you today?"

Some women would answer the door in a negligee and a garter. Some would dress up in heels. And I would say, "You look lovely. What do you like? Maybe a little massage?" You know, I'd try to feel it out.

Toni: What's the most important trait for an escort? Good looks? Intelligence? Personality?

Eric: Probably the looks and if you're hung big. Of course you have to be personable. But most women I've been with wanted someone well-hung, and I'm OK in that area.

Toni: Do you think women really want that? Does size matter?

Eric: I think it helps. After all, you never see small dildos, do you?

Toni: You mentioned that you think older women are more easy-going than younger ones. What else makes older women better?

Eric: They can show you some new things sometimes.

Dane: Like sexually?

Eric: Yeah. New tricks. And they're not shy. I don't think they're as shy as the younger girls. They don't mind coming right out and saying something. They're open. They want to get right to it quicker. They're better lovers than the younger women.

Dane: What kind of things did they teach you?

Eric: Well, one taught me this: she'd be riding up on top of me, and then she'd take her hand and put it on my dick, and then just ride up and down like that a little while. And she used to like then take her hands off and just slide all the way down. I mean, that's something I used to like.

Dane: Would you ever try the gay sex thing, if you were asked?

Eric: No. I mean, I've thought about it, because it's more money. But there's no way I could. No, not my style.

And the one time someone wanted to tie me up, I found myself really getting into it.

Toni: Was there ever anything they suggested that you said, "Hey, that's just not right for me?"

Eric: No, there was nothing that I wouldn't do with them.

Toni: The statistics are something like, more than fifty percent of married people cheat. Do you think that's true?

Eric: It's true. And I think it's higher than that.

Toni: Do you think it's hard to find a woman who's faithful?

Eric: Yeah. I know they're out there, but it's hard to find them. And I think that a lot of them, when they're ready to split up, they already got someone to go to. They get someone lined up.

Dane: Do you think women are more insecure than men in general?

Eric: No. I think it depends on their mothers and fathers.

If the father took and split on the mother for another woman, they're going to think when they get married, "Well, my husband is going to do that to me."

Dane: Well, if it's not insecurity, why do you think so many are cheating?

Eric: Variety. I think they want somebody new. They aren't satisfied at home.

Toni: Do you think it's OK if they're in a marriage and they're not being satisfied?

Eric: Yeah. Because as long as they made an attempt to try to work it out. Because it's all what you make of it. You can get aroused, you just have to do different things.

One woman, she says, "My husband would never get excited about me." I say, "Try to get some different toys, maybe go do it in the car somewhere." Different things, you know. It's all what you make of it.

Toni: So you feel if a woman has tried in her sex life with her husband and it's just not working, that basically it's OK to see an escort, rather than live a life of self-sacrifice or something? That she should at least be able to enjoy herself?

Eric: Yeah, I do.

Toni: Do you think a breakdown in a marriage stems first and foremost from the lack of communication?

Eric: Right.

Toni: And when that breaks down, the sexual part starts breaking down as well?

Eric: Oh, yeah.

Toni: Do you think that working as an escort has increased your self-esteem or decreased it?

Eric: I think it gave me a little more self-esteem. Because I felt like I was wanted. And I was surprised, too, because I don't think I'm super looking. But I guess, well, if you're well-hung enough, that's what counts, right?

Dane: Tell us about one of your favorite encounters.

Eric: It was in a bathtub. Bubbles and stuff, and it was all around her. And there were mirrors in the bathroom, and on the ceiling and the wall, everywhere mirrors. It was great. And I really felt aroused the whole time I was with this lady. A beautiful silver and white bathroom, and the music was playing. She had on a Gato Barbieri album, "Caliente," I think, and it was real special. I just wish I could remember her name.

Steve

Dane's Note: We met Steve through a contact at a health spa. He called and insisted on seeing us right away. An imposing figure, he is 6 feet 5 inches tall, 225 pounds and has wavy blond hair and compelling blue eyes. We interviewed him twice in Boston, once at a coffee shop in a posh downtown hotel and again at an elegant hotel in the suburbs.

This man was the skirt-chaser par excellence. When I left the interview a few times to get a drink, Steve lost no time coming on to Toni. He told her

repeatedly how beautiful she was, and even tried touching her knee under the
table. As he said many times during the interview, he is indeed "a very sexual
person."

Dane: Tell us about yourself, Steve.

Steve: Well, I played pro football for a couple of years. I was a tight end. I want to keep my privacy, obviously, so I won't name the team. Anyway, one Sunday I caught a pass up the middle, and when I got taken down, I fell on my hand. I broke my wrist and it never was the same after that. So my sports career ended before it really got started. Basically, I'm big and blond with that All-American look.

Toni: How did you get into the escort business?

Steve: I had a friend who was a big fan, and he said, "Look. You're big and tall. You're in the public eye. Would you be interested in escorting women to events? Political gatherings, that type of thing?"

The money sounded good and it seemed kind of exciting so I did it. Well, I never had a problem meeting women. When you play pro football it's so easy. They come to you. But now I was getting paid for it, and that was a new twist.

Dane: Is that when you decided this would be your new profession?

Steve: Yes. This friend of mine, it turned out that he owned a large escort agency. He started getting me more referrals, and, instead of just taking women out to functions, I was getting into the pure sexual part of the business. Now I was getting paid to go to bed with often-times incredible women.

Toni: Where did you work as an escort?

Steve: I started out on the West Coast. Then I went to Florida.

Dane: What made you set up business in Florida?

Steve: I heard from other escorts that a lot of business was available, especially in Palm Beach and Boca. I got a couple of referrals and started like that.

After a while, I was like, complete Tom Cruise in *Cocktail*. You know, the women he was with in that movie! I had more business than I could handle.

With most women, it was a fantasy for them to be with me because I was a pro ball player. I still wear my Divisional ring. See? It's a corporate tool, in a respect. It shows you're somebody. The ring is very large. You can't miss it. Women ask what it is. The door opens.

Also, I was always upscale both in my presentation and in my selection of clients. I always wore Armani suits and my best smile. Going to Florida and doing my thing here was a great move for me.

Toni: How often did you see these women?

Steve: There was one lady, Gina, I shacked up with her for three months. We stayed at her place in Aspen. I had my own four-wheel drive Jeep to use, the run of this incredible chalet and a free ski pass. Aspen is an interesting place. You know, the lifestyle of some of those people is really fucked up. They wake up in the morning and work out like crazy, ski all afternoon, and blow coke up their face all night. They do this day after day.

Anyway, Gina was really getting into this drug routine, and I was like, "Get me outta here." So I split.

Toni: For that three months, what did she pay you?

Steve: At the beginning, I told her I wanted two thousand dollars a week. For the first four or five weeks I collected that. But then she started to get screwed up on the coke, and the money wasn't there regularly. But in the end, I wound up making thousands plus all the perks. I wound up keeping the Jeep also.

It's interesting, you know. I have a couple of friends who were on the team with me at Boston College years ago. They're the dumbest doornails in the world, but they're set for life now because they played for that Cotton Bowl team with Doug Flutie. And that opens up all sorts of avenues and doors. It does. It's incredible.

Teammates of mine are now in sports broadcasting for major networks and it's not for what they know, but for who they are or were.

Toni: Did you find that a lot of woman had the attitude that they own you because they're paying for you?

Steve: All of them pretty much had that notion, but I didn't care. I was getting paid a thousand dollars a night. Let them have their fun, and I'll walk to the bank with the money.

Dane: Did you ever run an ad?

Steve: Yeah. My family is from Australia, so my ad said, "Tall handsome man, just arrived from Australia. Let me show you why they call it the land from down under." My phone was ringing off the hook.

I remember I got a call from this one woman. Her husband is a network TV producer who spends a lot of time in New York City. She had a red convertible Jaguar and she had this fantasy to get banged in this car. She called me her "fantasy dreamer." I did her bent over the back seat. She really enjoyed it because her husband owned the car and she hated the guy! He was physically abusive to her, and she wanted to get back at him.

Dane: What did you like best about the business?

Steve: Definitely the money. The excitement, also, you know, being with different women all the time. But the bottom line was the money. A guy can make one hundred and fifty thousand dollars a year, and I really like my work.

Toni: Were you ever in a situation where you thought the woman you were with was dangerous?

Steve: Yes. One time. I met this woman in a bar. We had a couple drinks, and we really hit it off and decided to take off and go to her place. I started driving and then she got crazy, pulled a knife out of her purse and started saying weird things and threatening me. I think she was on drugs. I calmed her down as much as I could, quickly pulled over at a convenience store and asked her to go inside and get me some cigarettes. As soon as I saw her go inside, I took off. I never saw her again. I left her in the middle of nowhere, and didn't give a damn. You know, I could have been stabbed or killed. That's as close to a dangerous woman as I ever want to get.

Toni: Do you feel there is good market out there for an escort? Are there a lot of women who want to hire men?

Steve: It's amazing just how many women are out there who want it. I mean, I got this one woman who's been calling. She's been dying to see me. She's like, "When am I gonna meet you? When am I gonna see you?" And I said, "Well, I'm really busy." She told me she's always wanted to be with a pro ball player, not to mention an Australian. She's like thirty-five years old, calls me every night. She's just dying for someone to come up and screw her.

I guess she thinks I'm a Choate sort of person, upper crust, you know, top of the echelon. Maybe she just has a fantasy about me.

Dane: Did you ever want to get involved emotionally with a client?

Steve: Oh, yeah. There was this one, her father owned the a big casino out in Vegas, a multibillionaire. She was adopted. She was twenty-seven, and she hired me because she was going to a ball, some country club event, and she wanted to be represented by someone a little better than a guy you'd find in a bar. So she hired me. She was wild and beautiful, and of course, rich. I pursued it for awhile, but it didn't pan out. Anyway, one of her fantasies was to date an escort.

I've had other beautiful women, too. In fact, I could write a book on how to find the young, the beautiful, and the rich. Since the 1600s, people have always thought men were more promiscuous than women, but that's not true. Men were just more visible about it.

I've done the party scene in Washington, D.C., you know. Escorts are everywhere, at all the big political events. The whole place would be filled with them. They're hired out. The tab is ten, twenty grand. It's paid by someone, and they just show up. That's for, like, ten escorts.

Toni: What do you feel are the negative aspects of being an escort?

Steve: Conscience. If you're a real person, you're conscience starts to talk to you. It comes in spurts. I mean, I think everybody has a degree of insanity. But most of us just know how to turn it on and turn it off. Same thing with escorts, you can learn to turn it on and turn it off. I mean, there's a large degree of uncertainty in it. For example, you two could be undercover agents instead of authors. You just never know.

Toni: Do you feel this line of work has helped you in being able to size people up instantly?

Steve: Oh, I got a natural gift for that. You find a pattern of honesty, see if they're bullshitting, see if they contradict themselves.

Toni: Who do you feel has the power in an encounter between an escort and the woman who hires him?

Steve: Usually the women, but I don't ever let them get too much power. You can't.

Dane: Are drugs still such a part of the business?

Steve: Major! Especially in Palm Beach. It was always a part of the date because it heightens the enjoyment, you know?

Toni: Did the women buy you gifts?

Steve: Oh, yeah. Gold chains. And I don't wear gold, so I'd end up just giving it away. Clothes. They'd buy me Armani suits, top shelf stuff.

Toni: At these public events, how did the women who hired you introduce you?

Steve: Some would say, "My nephew," "My friend," "My date for the evening." They never wanted people to know.

Toni: Didn't people know anyway? I mean, weren't you much younger than many of the women you escorted?

Steve: Yes, and of course other people knew what was really going on.

Dane: Were you ever at one of those parties with a client and saw a woman you wanted to date?

Steve: Sure. Even when I was at one of those big parties with a woman, I'd be canvassing the place for a young girl I could hook up with. A lot of those ladies would hold on to you, make sure you're right by their side, not straying. And I've always had a tendency to stray, you see.

Toni: Do you feel other men are threatened by what you do?

Steve: Oh, yeah. But I think mainly they're jealous. They're envious because I played ball. And add to that, that I'm now an escort.

Toni: What are the Palm Beach women like?

Steve: Very arrogant. They think women rule.

Toni: Isn't that true?

Steve: Ha! Well, with all that money behind them, they sure do have an attitude. Actually, the mediocre ones are worse than the beautiful ones. Probably because they are mediocre. They need the power. The beautiful ones knew that they were beautiful. Kind of like yourself, Toni. You know you're beautiful, don't you?

Toni: When you're doing a book, you can ask the questions, Steve. In the meantime, let's get on with the interview.

Steve: OK.

Toni: When you were with these women, what was the conversation like? What subjects did you talk about?

Steve: Me. What I did. The sports. It was all about me.

Dane: One of the things we've been hearing from escorts is that older women are better lovers. How do you feel about that?

Steve: Older women are better lovers. They know what they want. And they aim to please.

Toni: Just out of curiosity, are there really a lot of groupies that follow pro sports players?

Steve: It's the most unbelievable thing you've ever seen. I mean, these girls, they wait at the hotels from city to city. After a while you just get to know them by name. There are always women around when you're somebody.

There's just a huge amount of groupies out there. I played special teams, didn't even start, but because I was with that group, I could have any woman I wanted. And you don't even have to be on the team. Because now, I can still do the same thing.

Dane: Tell us more about the parties you've been to as an escort.

Steve: Well, political parties down in D.C. were pretty much of a trip. I saw most of it first-hand. As far as women and fantasies, I escorted this woman who had 44DD breasts. I mean, I have small hands and small feet but I was gifted with something else. And, anyway, her husband was this tiny thin guy. So she always had this fantasy about having a "titty fuck." That's all she wanted.

Toni: Do you like the "jock" label?

Steve: Yeah, I do.

Dane: How did you run your business?

Steve: Very discreetly. Had an answering service screen all the calls. Escorting is great if you do it right. I do this for the money and for the kick, you know?

Dane: Tell us about the women you were with.

Steve: All very rich. And because of how that ad read, being Australian and how I can show them why they call it the land from down under, all these women who saw my ad were expecting me to go down on them. Incidentally, women love that. All women love it.

Toni: Do you ever have a moral issue with being an escort?

Steve: Of course I do. But everyone has a moral issue with everything they do in life, don't they?

Toni: If you had a younger brother who wanted to be an escort, would you advise him to go for it?

Steve: Sure. Why not? I got a friend right now who's dying to do it. He might even get into porn movies. Do safe sex videos, that kind of stuff.

Dane: What are safe sex videos?

Steve: It's a major market. Movies in the form of pornos except with condoms. I mean, the major porn stars, they're all dying of AIDS. Something has to be done. A lot of those stars aren't even good-looking. I guess you don't have to be.

Toni: How important do you think looks are to an escort?

Steve: Very important. Because the fantasy is really what you're supplying. You're the knight in armour. You gotta look the part. What do you go for, Toni? Looks?

Toni: I go for intelligence.

Steve: Intelligence? I mean, what if he had an I.Q. higher than anybody in the world but was a dog to look at?

Toni: Well I try not to judge by looks. I find that someone who is intelligent tends to become better looking, and someone who is not intelligent, I don't tend to see as attractive.

Steve: Oh, I agree. But I think most people look at looks first. I mean, everything is done on first impression. Most women, the first question they ask me on the phone is: "Are you good looking?"

Toni: So when they ask you to describe yourself, what do you say?

Steve: If I'm feeling cocky, I tell them I'm 6 feet 5 inches, I'm in very good shape, 225 pounds of sex appeal. When I played ball, I was 250 pounds. I think women judge by looks as much as men do. Some women even ask how long you are!

Toni: Do you feel that you are living out the American male fantasy?

Steve: Oh, yeah. Definitely. I got buddies who'd give anything to do what I do.

I make it a point to go out of my way to help my women, make sure they have a good time, I please them in every way I can. I'm sure I've been taken advantage of from time to time. I'm a nice guy and it happens. I mean, I got dumped on my face last summer by a girl I was going to marry. I was with her three years.

Dane: What happened?

Steve: Well, in the beginning when I was with her, I was attracted to some other women. I was finding that tough, but I tried to put blinders on so I wouldn't wander. But along the way there was these girls coming at me that were like, fifteens on a scale of one to ten, intelligent, bright and gorgeous, and they were all over me, flooding me with attention and affection. So this girl ended up standing me up four days before the wedding.

Toni: Because of the other women in your life?

Steve: Yeah. And the thing is, they were really just good friends. But she didn't see it that way. We'd go out and dance and stuff. That was it. I'm the type of guy when I go out, I'm friendly. I meet people. I have a great time. A lot of times, girls will come over to me, ask me to dance, and after I dance with them, they'll think I'm their property, you know? Then I'll go talk to other girls and they don't like that at all.

I think my girlfriend was pretty insecure. She came from a dysfunctional family.

Toni: What was your family like?

Steve: My father was an alcoholic. But he hasn't had a drink in twenty years. My family is very rigid, very Catholic. Life is basically normal, no real surprises.

Toni: Coming from such a conservative background, do you think your decision to become an escort had anything to do with rebellion?

Steve: No. I'm a complete cut above other people. And I'm putting a lot of money in my pocket to boot. You should see me out, Toni, I'm like David Letterman. I'm a natural for this business. I have a good stage presence.

Toni: Do you think that's important?

Steve: It's important to make other people happy, yeah.

Toni: Why?

Steve: Because there's people less fortunate than me. I'm a Big Brother. I work for charitable functions. God gave me a great natural talent to play football. I'm a natural athlete. It's my way of giving back.

Dane: Did women like the fact that you were Australian?

Steve: Oh, yeah. They have this Mel Gibson thing. Incidentally, that outback accent that you hear is actually not all that common. We don't all speak like that, "shrimp on the barbie" and stuff.

Dane: Would the women describe themselves to you over the phone?

Steve: Sure. But of course everyone sounds great over the phone. For example, when a woman tells you she's got olive skin, you know she's fat. It's like when a friend tells you he's got this girl for you. She's got a great personality. You know she's ugly.

Dane: What kind of questions would you ask them?

Steve: Screening out questions. Like how their work day was, if they worked. Do they like the arts? Do they travel? One thing I'd never ask, though: "Are you married?" I never asked that. It wasn't any of my business. I didn't want to know.

Dane: How many women that you escorted to functions did you actually sleep with?

Steve: Well, in a year's time, I'd maybe escort sixty women to functions, and I didn't go to bed with all of them either.

Toni: Did some of them want the date to end in sex and you declined?

Steve: Yeah. But the thing is, I can get hard any time I want. I've always been very sexually aggressive. I lost my virginity at age nineteen with a girl on a beach. She just devoured me right there on the beach.

Toni: Did your fiancé know about your life as an escort?

Steve: No, I never told her. And it bothered me because I wanted to be open with her. If she was an open-minded individual, I would have told her.

Toni: If she had told you that she had been an escort, would that have bothered you?

Steve: I don't think so.

Dane: Have you ever been hired by a couple?

Steve: Once. I saw an ad: "Mature white couple wants single male," so I called it. The guy called, wanted me to send photos, and what he wanted was for me to screw his wife while he masturbated. It didn't do anything for me, but I figured I'd try it once. Once was enough.

But as an escort, generally you have a great time. If you're sexual enough, good looking, and a good conversationalist like me, you can make money. I read all the time, *Newsweek, Time, Wall Street.*

When I walk into a bar, I see the heads turn. Women sigh, check me out.

Dane: Can you remember some of your first experiences as an escort?

Steve: I was nervous, sweating. She was fifty-four, could have been my mother, working class, not attractive. Wanted dinner, wanted me to sleep with her. I thought I had to sleep with her, so I did. It wasn't a good sight.

She didn't want me to wear a condom; she wanted the real feeling. I'm not bragging, but they don't make them big enough for me anyway. And they squeeze me so hard I don't ejaculate. And women want that natural feeling anyway.

So I'm with this older woman, I'm pounding her into the pavement. I just wanted her to have her orgasm so I could go. It was a bad scene.

She was like, saggy, and here I was thinking, "God, what am I doing here?" You gotta understand, I'm a pro ball player!

The next woman was nicer. Her name was Caroline. Seems like those real nice women always had those real nice, fancy Southern names, like Caroline, Tammy. They don't have names like Sue or Beth. They've got names with flare.

Dane: How did you get paid?

Steve: I got paid by the escort agency, not by the woman. But I always got tips. I was averaging like two hundred and fifty dollars an hour. I was amazed because I played pro ball, and was making only thirty-five thousand dollars a year. And here were these women, giving me three hundred dollar tips! That's just tips!

And they'd thank me, saying, "I had a fantastic time. I'd love to see you again."

Now keep in mind, they were tipping me three hundred dollars just for my company! I mean, a lot of these women, I escorted them to events and we did nothing else. No sex was involved.

Toni: What do you think women want?

Steve: They wanted tenderness. They wanted me to tell them how attractive they were. We would go from one conversation to another, but I didn't care. It would eat up the time.

It was almost like I was doing phone sex. Trying to eat up as much time as I could to get paid as much money as I could.

Toni: What are women doing with escorts that they can't do with their husbands?

Steve: Well, often they married the wrong man. They settled for second best, you know? Some wanted oral sex. They're husbands wouldn't do it. Some were with men who were tiny, you know? And I'd talk dirty to them. A lot of women liked that. I'd say, "Oh, you're so hot, so incredible." And just go on and on. These women were like, scratching the skin off my back. It was unbelievable. And I just kept pumping them full of the sex talk, you know?

Some women wanted me to masturbate on them and come all over their face. And I mean, I've got this innate sex drive, you know? I can come four times in one night.

Toni: Which makes this profession very good for you.

Steve: Very good. You know, there was this one guy I know, a professor. His wife was the sexiest, hottest thing in the world. Blond, she kind of looked like you, Toni. She has this sexy yet innocent look.

Toni: You're very good, Steve. Very smooth.

Steve: So anyway, this professor told me an average male comes three thousand times in his life. And then dries up. And frankly, I think I've reached that peak.

But anyway, the truth is, I really respect women. A lot of guys in the business don't. But I do, I really do.

Dane: What was one of your most exciting encounters?

Steve: I had an experience with a woman and her daughter. She was about forty, her daughter, twenty-one.

Dane: What happened?

Steve: We had the wildest time. The mother and I had dinner, we came home, sat down. I was smoking a joint, doing speed, doing coke. I was wired. Anyway, in walks her daughter. The woman says, "Steve, I'd like to introduce you to my daughter. This is my daughter Dawn." Me and Dawn started hitting it off, and her mother got pissed. Like she was getting jealous. I mean, she just came over, sat on my lap, straddled me and started kissing me. And her daughter was right there. She just sat there and watched. Man, this was the type of escort date I liked!

So her mother's kissing me, and I was rubbing her back, putting my hands down her pants. And her daughter's sitting over there in a skirt, and I put my hand out and started rubbing her daughter's legs, fingering her. It was great.

I did everything imaginable. Every sexual position, every sexual desire. I did them both twice, I ate them, licked them, did everything. That's a big fantasy, you know, the mother-daughter thing. I was hired by the mother; probably should have got more money for doing the daughter, too!

I figured, "What do I have to lose?" I thought the mother would tell me to leave her daughter alone. A lot of guys dream of two women, but a mother and daughter! That's an even bigger fantasy. You read about it in *Penthouse*. I'm living it.

Dane: What kind of requests have you turned down?

Steve: I've turned down being blindfolded and tied to the bed. Because I always want to know what's going on. I always want to be in control. I never want to let down my guard.

Toni: Do you think sex is about control?

Steve: Sure it is. It's about control when it's sex. But when sex is love, it's about love. I suppose that's rather romantic, coming from an escort.

Toni: What are you looking for in life?

Steve: Well, I don't know. I don't know if I'll ever get married. I love children. I'd like to have one of my own, but I think that's not going to happen for a while. Right now the money, excitement, and the variety are enough.

Toni: Would you tell the next woman you become involved with that you're an escort?

Steve: I'd let them know up front that some times I'm going to be called on to perform as an escort. But honest to God, I'm a very sexual person.

Toni: What is a "very sexual person?"

Steve: If I could get laid every night, I would. And I can get laid every night.

Toni: Don't you think most people can?

Steve: No. Not most guys. A lot of guys can't. I see guys struggle bad. But I'm a very sexual person. For me it's pretty easy.

Toni: So this is the perfect profession for you?

Steve: I think I'm made for it.

Toni: What if one of these women offered you the position of a "kept man?" She'll take you all over the world. She'll wine and dine you. She'll pay for everything. Would you do it?

Steve: Sure. I mean, isn't everything today run by a price tag?

Toni: Do you think more men cheat or more women?

Steve: Men. Women are more committed. It's just innate.

Toni: Who has the higher sex drive, men or women?

Steve: Women. They last longer. Women peak mid-thirties, men peak at eighteen. Well, there are a few exceptions. I mean, I haven't peaked. I have a long way to go!

The European Tradition

The gold-digging playboy of the fifties had his historical predecessors in seventeenth century England: a dazzling army of dandies who, with looks, charm and exquisite manners, exploited libidinous aristocratic women.

Writing in 1709, Sir Richard Steele said of Beau Fielding, the most notorious ladies' man of the day, "woman was his mistress, and the whole sex his seraglio."

Political turmoil spawned the British fortune chasers after King Charles I was executed in 1649 by a parliament fed up with subsidizing the spendthrift House of Stuart. When the monarchy was abolished, spoiled young Royalists fled their native land to live in exile in France where they enthusiastically embraced the excesses of the French court.

Nine years later, back in England, the Puritan Commonwealth fell apart. In 1660, Charles II ascended the throne and the exiled aristocrats returned to England. Dressed in the elaborate style of the French Musketeers, they arrived sporting flowing lace cuffs and lavish ruffles, silk stockings, bejeweled buttons and buckles, hats with long ostrich plumes, sashes, gloves, and square-toed, high-heeled shoes. Wig, cape and sword, too, were *de rigeur*. Foppish, posturing, blue blooded clotheshorses became the darlings of the English noblewomen.

Calling themselves *beaux* (from the French word "handsome") they ran through their own family funds then turned to wealthy women for financial relief. Like the American heiresses of the Industrial Age to come, privileged English women in the seventeenth century with time on their hands and money to burn amused themselves with dashing young men.

England was not an isolated case. The attentive man who made his living keeping company with women was a staple all over Europe, often in the employ of the women's husbands. A century later in France, men of means often paid other men to watch over their wives (no doubt while these libertines engaged in the amorous pursuits common to their liberal era.) Like the 1960s, their period was considered a sexual revolution although it wasn't called that. French gentlemen-in-waiting were called *chevaliers servants*. They came from a class of penniless nobles or priests and survived by their wit and charm until the ladies tired of them and turned their gaze elsewhere.

Meanwhile, the upper-class Italian counterpart of the *beaux* and *chevalier servant* was the cicisbeo. The double standard was more evident in Italy.

Morals were lax for men but the Italian husband kept his wife on a short leash. To guard her from the attentions of other men, a husband would hire an escort, a *cicisbeo*. (Cassell's Italian Dictionary gives gigolo as a translation of *cicisbeo*.)

The *cicisbeo* catered to his lady's every need, spending the entire day at her side. According to Maurice Vaussard's *Daily Life in Eighteenth Century Italy*, "the *cicisbeo*, or *cavaliere servente*, was never a lover, although he was allowed to attend his lady's toilet in the morning while her hair was done and her maids dressed her." (Given his duties, the *cicisbeo* might be suspected of doing more than just looking.)

After the lady's toilet, the two would lunch together and then spend the afternoon making social visits. In keeping with the custom of the time, the husband and wife dined together. However, as soon as the evening meal was over, the couple went their separate ways, she to the theater or opera with her *cicisbeo*, he to his mistress.

The Italian husband, glaringly inattentive, at least tried to make sure his wife was never lonely, but he never let go of the reins. He chose her companion for her and paid for his services and only the husband could dismiss him. Wealthy Italian women had little opportunity to set the terms of the relationship with their husbands but they did have a consolation prize in their attentive *cicisbeo*.

Jean-Pierre

Jean-Pierre is educated, well–spoken, pleasant but rather average in appearance, and classically French. We spent about three hours with him at a quiet bar in Washington, D.C., having met him through an attorney with political connections. Cosmopolitan and debonair, he speaks several languages and is working toward his master's degree.

Jean-Pierre displayed the same characteristic we had observed in the other escorts: an ability to charm women.

Dane: Can you give us your background?

Jean-Pierre: I got a scholarship to the *Institut d'Etudes Politiques* in Paris and I was first in my class, also *magna cum laude* in my college in the United States. I studied at the University of Miami for my M.B.A. before I came here to Washington, D.C. I'm from am upper middle class family in Europe.

Toni: How did you get started as an escort?

Jean-Pierre: I was living in Paris. I had left home at eighteen to be independent. I was in school and needed money. Rent is very high in Paris, the food is expensive, a Coca Cola costs you four dollars in Paris. I needed money. I was doing some modeling, teaching kung fu part time, and I worked as a bouncer in a nightclub.

The nightclub I worked at was Bains Douches, a very famous club in Paris. One night Bianca Jagger came over to party and she had a whole following with her; one of them was interested in me.

This friend approached me and wanted to go out that same night. She wanted to have sex with me. I was nervous because I had been told that I shouldn't have a relationship with anyone in the club, since I was a bouncer.

Then she said, "Listen, listen. I'll pay you," and this was the first time it occurred to me that I could actually get paid for doing this. She was about twenty-three years old, and I think she was on drugs because no sane woman would do that. I mean, it was 3 a.m., and this place had been a strip joint previously. The people that go there now are very artistic jet setters.

So I thought, "Why not?" One night's pay as a bouncer was one hundred dollars, and I said to her jokingly, "How much?" And she said, "Anything you want." I didn't know, so I said twenty-five hundred francs, which at the time was about two hundred and fifty American dollars.

So I thought, "Wow, I will make almost four hundred dollars tonight just for working as a bouncer and having sex. All I have to do is make sure she enjoys herself."

The club closed at 5 a.m., and we went to her hotel. She offered me cocaine. I said I didn't do drugs. She took some drugs, we had sex, and, at that point, she said, "Here's your money."

I said, "No, no I was just joking around." She said, "Take it. Take it." And since I needed the money because I was a student, I accepted it.

Then I started thinking, " Why not try to do this through an escort service?" Then you have a boss, or patron, the guy who takes care of getting you clients.

So I went to an agency and they interviewed me. They asked what sexual orientation I was because obviously there are services for men as well as women. I said, "I don't want to do men. I want to do women."

Then he said if I wanted to try that, fine, but that I'd make a whole lot more money doing men. I told him I was not into sexual deviancy; I'd stick with women.

So I waited. And I waited about a month and a half. Finally one day he called and said, "Listen. I got a call from a woman. She's sixty-two years old, a widow who's lonely. I know you are well-educated and cultured; all you have to do is go there and make her feel good."

I asked about her financial background since I was doing this for the money. Some people will say, "Money's not important." No, it's not important to those who have it. But I wanted an education, and that costs money.

He told me she was wealthy. Upper society. I said, "How much do you think I could get from her?" He said, "Let's ask for a thousand francs." He said, "I'll take half since I am your broker and you take the other half." And that was the first job I did.

Toni: What was it like, being with a sixty-two-year-old woman when you were eighteen?

Jean-Pierre: Strange. First of all, I'd never dated anyone older than me, except for that friend of Bianca Jagger's.

Toni: Were you nervous?

Jean-Pierre: Not nervous. Kind of disgusted, actually. I mean, she was a good-looking sixty-two-year-old, but she was sixty-two. Of course, the dream is you find the sixty-two-year-old that looks like Joan Collins, right? But no, that wasn't the case.

Dane: What was going on in your mind?

Jean-Pierre: I thought, "OK. For the love of money, no. But for the necessity of money, I will do this."

Toni: So what happened next?

Jean-Pierre: I talked to this woman for three hours before I put a hand on her. It took me that amount of time to make myself feel comfortable. I asked about her husband, and she got all nervous. She didn't want to talk about him because he had passed away. So I talked to her about her grandchildren. She told me their ages, about my age, and I felt uncomfortable and thought, "My God, I'm having sex with my grandmother!"

Dane: What was her reaction when you started to touch her?

Jean-Pierre: She would say, "Oh, I'm old. Finished. My life is over." I wanted her to feel good. After three hours I had begun to feel sorry for her.

Toni: What did you tell her to make her feel more comfortable?

Jean-Pierre: That she still had quite a few good years ahead of her, she should enjoy herself. That she was still attractive.

Then she showed me a picture of herself, when she was young, in a bathing suit. We began talking about her, how pretty she had been, the places she had seen, things she had done.

And then I asked what she misses about being married. She said, "The support. Especially the sexual support." So I said, "Specifically, what do you miss?"

She told me she misses being held, being gently taken care of, you know, "taken to the clouds." In French, it sounds better, you see.

Then we talked about what she would like me to do, if such and such a thing felt good and, little by little, I found myself becoming more macho about this, losing my fear about being paid for this.

Then I started getting into it. I felt like "The French Lover, By Appointment Only."

Toni: You were starting to feel excited by her?

Jean-Pierre: Yes. I would touch her hand, kiss her arm, and she would say, "Oh, it's been such a long, long time." I would say, "Tonight you're all mine. I'm going to take care of you."

It was all going to my head. I was getting into it. You see, you have to separate the fact that you're getting paid for it and concentrate on the fact that, simply, she is the woman and you are the man.

Dane: So now, she feels more comfortable. What happens next?

Jean-Pierre: We started undressing. As I undressed her, I would compliment her on the breasts, the softness of her skin, the beauty of her eyes, the hardness of the nipples. All these things that I thought would make her more comfortable. And then she just laid back and sighed softly, and I knew what that meant. I had seen the movie *Breathless*, and I remembered the scene with ice.

Toni: What happened with that scene?

Jean-Pierre: It was steamy, romantic. And I acted it out in her hotel room.

I thought that if I rubbed ice on her, the wrinkles would disappear, the nipples would get harder. She would appear more youthful. And it worked!

Her skin became more taut, more young-looking. And I whispered, "Look, you are being rejuvenated! It is because you are destined to be loved by a man like me tonight!"

Obviously, it's just a reaction: when you rub with cold, the nipples will harden. But I said, "Look, you are becoming young!"

Toni: How did she react to what you were saying?

Jean-Pierre: She started to believe it. Then as we were lying on the couch, I gently took down her pants.

Then I made a mistake. I said, "What would you like us to do? Go in the other room? Stay here?" She got nervous and demanded, "Why are you asking me this?" I said, "What?" She said, "You know, you're making me feel like I'm paying you!"

Of course, she was paying me, but I wasn't supposed to act like it.

Toni: Is that a problem for women? That they feel like the escort is being paid to be with them?

Jean-Pierre: Sure. The reason clients called me back is because I would make them forget that this is a client/boss relationship. I learned that with this woman. I had asked, "What would you like me to do?" She got upset because it made it sound like I was being paid for it; like I was a hired hand. That's not the kind of thing you'd say in bed to your wife or girlfriend. It's not natural.

There is a difference between performing and being spontaneous.

Jack Nicholson, in the movie *A Few Good Men*, was not acting like the colonel. He was the colonel. I had been acting like a lover, not being a lover.

Dane: What did you do to salvage the evening with this older woman?

Jean-Pierre: I had to start again and for an hour we were talking again. I told her, "I'm sorry. You're the first woman I've ever been with under these circumstances."

And then I thought, "Oh, this is a good line, that this is the first woman I've been with. Maybe I can use it next time with the next woman, too."

Anyway, she started warming up again. So I went on, "I'm a young man, only eighteen. I'm just trying to pay for my education. I think you are a wonderful woman. Please don't take offense. I don't really know what to do. This is my first time."

Eventually, she forgave me.

Dane: Did you pick up where you left off?

Jean-Pierre: Yes. This time I put the ice on her legs, on the private places. And this time I didn't say anything; I just took her. I gently pried open her legs, rubbed the ice there, and to my surprise, it wasn't that bad, that area, even though she was sixty-two. I was expecting to see a pumpkin or prune, and I was surprised that it was so nice. I enjoyed the evening.

And you know, I learned the thing about giving pleasure is, anyone can give it to anyone. It just takes time and a little understanding.

Toni: Are you still working as an escort here in D.C.?

Jean-Pierre: Yes, the business still excites me. I know enough about it now that it is effortless. I have my clientele, which is six regular women. There are no surprises. I have a very comfortable life.

Dane: What kind of clientele do you have? Since this is the political hub of the country, do you have liaisons with some interesting women?

Jean-Pierre: Some are very interesting. I have recently been with a senator's wife. You would know the name if I told you, but of course I can't say. Generally the women who see me are in their forties and fifties, in somewhat unhappy marriages. They have lots of money and what seems like insatiable sex drives.

And because they are connected with politicians, they are often articulate, charming, very much the perfect hostesses. For the most part, they are very desirable.

Dane: Are there many escorts working in D.C.?

Jean-Pierre: Many, it seems. The business here is more of an upscale version than some cities.

Toni: Is there an opportunity for the aspiring gigolo to make a good living here?

Jean-Pierre: Yes, I think so. When I started here a couple of years ago, I turned down many women. You see, I didn't want a large clientele. Yes, there are still many women available. As long as the politicians are so busy making the laws, there will be women waiting for escorts.

Dane: How sexually experienced were you when you became an escort?

Jean-Pierre: By the time I had that first encounter, at age eighteen, I had been with about sixty girls. Like Aristotle said, "We are all just animals with two legs." In fact, when you look at a woman walking down the street, well-dressed, cool, attaché case, Rolex, this same person can be sprawled in a supine position during sex, on four legs, groveling, clawing, screaming. Yet, it's the same person.

Everybody's like this, an animal underneath. I mean, the sixty-two-year-old, she was old. A grandmother! And here she was, acting like an animal. And that's what I thought of when I was with other women. How they'd be out in public and then how the woman would be acting in private with me. The more conventional the woman is in real life, the more excited I get.

Dane: Do you use contraceptives?

Jean-Pierre: Always.

Toni: After the meeting with the first woman, how did you feel?

Jean-Pierre: Uncomfortable. I wanted to leave. But of course I had to stay and talk with her.

Toni: What kind of things did you talk with her about afterwards?

Jean-Pierre: I complimented her sexually. Told her I'd never felt so excited in my life. Obviously, that wasn't true. But when you're making love, it's very easy to say things you don't mean. The truth is, no matter how callous it may sound, when you're having sex, it's very easy to say "I love you."

Dane: How many women were you with in France that paid you?

Jean-Pierre: Twelve. All over forty-five years old.

Toni: OK, the million dollar question. American men versus European men. Who are the better lovers?

Jean-Pierre: Frenchmen are much better lovers. Women tell me I am more receptive to what they want than American men. Their wants and likes are very important to me. American men, they think their size is so important. But just because you are big, it doesn't mean you know how to use it. It doesn't mean she'll enjoy it. I think American men don't know this. They are concerned for their own pleasure. And this is what will always make the Frenchman the better lover.

Dane: What do you think of American women?

Jean-Pierre: They like football players, sports stars. Intellectuals in America don't spark women's interest.

Dane: How many times have you had sex in one day?

Jean-Pierre: Nine. I did it nine times in a day once.

Toni: The women who pay you, what has your longest relationship been with any of them?

Jean-Pierre: I saw one of them for eight months. She was forty-eight. She would never tell me her last name or where she lived or even her phone number. I had to page her. All I knew about her was that her husband traveled a lot. And that she loved sex a lot. And she needed things done to her that her husband wouldn't do.

Dane: For example?

Jean-Pierre: Anal sex. And I'd been doing that since I was fifteen. I was with a very odd French girl at that time. She wanted to be a virgin for her wedding night. Every time I tried to have sex with her, she said, "No, no!" She was only thirteen. So we had anal sex together for a year. A whole year! After that year, my best friend had sex with her and took her virginity anyway.

Toni: Why did you want to talk with us, Jean-Pierre?

Jean-Pierre: Because I want people to know, that *anybody*, anybody in my same situation, trying to raise a lot of money for something, would have done what I did.

And the women I was with, they have education. They're well-traveled. They have husbands and children and sometimes grandchildren, like anybody else.

Toni: What kind of money can guys make as escorts?

Jean-Pierre: I know guys here who make twenty thousand dollars a month.

Toni: How is it different working as an escort in France?

Jean-Pierre: Well, for one thing, escorts pay taxes. And it's mostly men who run the escort agencies.

Dane: Have you had clients that were absolutely gorgeous?

Jean-Pierre: Yes. When I saw this one woman, I couldn't believe it. She was beautiful! I said, "What are you doing here? Why do you need an escort?"

Dane: What did she say?

Jean-Pierre: She said, "Listen. I don't want to go through the hassle of having to pick up men because I'm a married woman. I have children. I don't want to be seen in the bar scene. I don't want to be in the singles scene. I would feel unfaithful if I would do that.

With you, we love each other physically, but it's for money. There is no moral guilt at all. When my husband comes home, I feel that I love him and there's no problem. It's just like when I close my eyes and pleasure myself. It's the same thing, being with an escort.

But out in the singles world, people see me, they talk, and if someone called, what would he say: 'Hello, Joanie, can I talk to your mother?' I mean, that would never work!

I just want to have my sexual desires fulfilled, and I don't want to pay the moral price for it."

Toni: If you were married and picked someone up in a bar, would you consider that immoral?

Jean-Pierre: Oh, I think so. You're married, you don't need to do that!

Now in Barcelona, they have clubs where married people go. It's ten dollars to get in. They have drinks, the people talk to each other, and after two or three hours someone will say, "Hey, I like your wife. Do you like mine? Well, let's all go upstairs." It's a big business over there.

It's just different in France. I mean, President Mitterrand had thirteen mistresses. Here, someone has a mistress, it's the end of the world.

Anyway, with these swinger clubs, the problem is that, just like the singles scene, people can be found out. And that is bad for the children. So, in my country, we avoid it. That's why a woman would go to a man like me.

Dane: Did you find that a lot of women wanted to do role-playing?

Jean-Pierre: A few. One wanted to pretend she was the nurse and I was the soldier going to war. She wanted to re-enact *For Whom the Bell Tolls* or something. She had read the book, I'm sure.

Then one woman wanted me to be the politician, and I was her political assistant. Kind of like an aide or something. She murmured words in Italian to me.

Toni: Did you enjoy the role-playing?

Jean-Pierre: Not really. Too much bullshit. I would rather a woman just comes right out and says, "My husband is away on work. I'm lonely. I need to be loved."

Dane: What do you think makes a good male escort? It's gotta be more than good looks.

Jean-Pierre: I will have you know I never once mentioned, since I started, about being physically good-looking. I didn't say that.

Obviously, you can't be repulsive. You have to be at least average in looks. But I think it's more important to be intelligent, well-traveled, and receptive. And the kind of man who caters to a woman.

If you are all these things, she will feel wonderful. Let's face it. A lot of women are married to very handsome men yet they are unhappy. So it's more than looks.

Toni: Did you ever become emotionally attached to a client?

Jean-Pierre: No. This I would never allow myself to do. If I feel I am losing myself to her, I simply stop seeing her. This is for money. And there is always another woman.

Maurice

We were sitting outside a hotel on South Beach in Miami talking about our book when a woman at the next table overheard us and said, "I think I have someone you'd like to talk to. His name is Maurice."

At the same trendy outdoor cafe we met Maurice. His French accent was so thick we had trouble understanding him at times.

It was easy, however, to see why women would be attracted to him — that European panache! His rugged, blond good looks and the way he softly whispers flowery French phrases comparing a woman to a goddess give him all the skills necessary for many more successful years in the business.

Toni: How did you get started as an escort?

Maurice: I came here to America and I was looking for an easy way to make some money. I saw some ads in the *New Times Magazine* in Miami where escorts were advertising, so I decided to put one in. This was two or three years ago. And then I started getting calls. It started as work; in the end I was doing it for fun.

Dane: What kind of response did you get to this ad?

Maurice: Maybe a hundred women, but I picked three, and they all became long-term relationships. I saw them once a week for about a year. They were all married.

Toni: What did your ad say?

Maurice: "Educated Frenchman, new in town, ready to be your companion." Something like that.

Dane: What would they say when they'd call?

Maurice: Something like, "I saw your ad. Can we see each other? Can we meet somewhere?"

Toni: What kind of place did you usually meet in?

Maurice: A dark, secluded, little restaurant near South Beach. Very intimate, romantic.

Toni: Tell us about the women who called. What were they like?

Maurice: In their forties. They wanted to get away from their home, try something new. Some of them just wanted companionship. They wanted to be in the company of an educated man, with manners and everything. That's what they expected. Of the women who called, I screened them down to nine, then met them and, finally, selected three.

Dane: What was a typical date?

Maurice: Restaurant, a drink somewhere, then they'd follow me home.

Toni: If you felt that a woman was unattractive, would you still go through with it?

Maurice: Yes, I would still spend the evening. But perhaps just as a friend. Some of them just needed to talk.

Dane: Were the women wealthy?

Maurice: Very! That's the only kind I'd see. Some of the women came from money; most married into it. One of them was married to a high profile C.E.O. in Miami. They had the summer home in Vermont, the chateau in France, and the house on Biscayne Bay.

One of them was married to a very wealthy Swede who had a collection of antique cars including an Auburn Boattail 1936 and even a Mercedes Gullwing, which I got to drive! And they had a yacht and several homes.

And one of them was married to a citrus grower. They had the ski lodge in Sun Valley, Idaho and a collection of antique toy soldiers.

Toni: Tell us about the first woman, the one married to the C.E.O. What was she like?

Maurice: Tall, shoulder-length red hair, forty-two, nice skin. She made a date with me for five days. Of course, she wanted more than companionship.

Toni: Five days is a long date. What did you charge?

Maurice: A thousand dollars a day. It was a cruise to Providenciales in the Turks and Caicos Islands.

Dane: Why did she answer your ad?

Maurice: She wanted an affair. She thought this was the best way to keep it secret.

Dane: What happened?

Maurice: She became emotionally attached to me. I didn't mind because I was making a lot of money, and she was very nice. But I wasn't in love with her. She wanted me to move closer to her home. Said she'd get me a penthouse nearby and pay for everything.

I had become very, very spoiled. I'm a Frenchman. I like the finer things. I'm a wine connoisseur. She bought me any wines I wanted. I'm partial to old Bordeaux and Burgundies. She gave me race car driving lessons. And then, there was the Rolex and the Mercedes.

Toni: Why didn't you accept the penthouse?

Maurice: It is a question of pride, no? You are with her, and then after awhile, she thinks she owns you. To accept would be to cross the line.

Toni: To a lot of women, being with a handsome Frenchman sounds very exciting. It's a fantasy. Did you find this to be true?

Maurice: Oh, yes. These American men, they are rude. They do not have much education. No "joie de vivre." No manners, no class. Here I am, a Frenchman. I know how to be with a woman.

If you want my opinion, to be a good walker or escort, we call them "walkers" in France, you need education and manners. The second thing is: Don't tell her your problems; listen to hers.

Dane: When a woman would answer your ad, would you discuss price?

Maurice: Oh, no, no! That's too American, too gauche. I would bring up the subject of money later.

Toni: Why didn't you go with an escort agency?

Maurice: They close as fast as they open. First, they're not run by professional people, in general. Second, the way they treat you, that is not always good.

Dane: Do escort agencies operate out of an office?

Maurice: No. Usually from apartments. A couple of people answering phone calls. There's a couple of phones and a few tables, very bare. When they're shut down, they simply open up under another name.

Toni: Tell us about the second woman you saw in a long-term relationship.

Maurice: She was very, very rich. Married to a multi-millionaire. She didn't have to work, of course, and she was bored all day long. The husband was older, had a big business, no time to worry about the wife. So, she would send a limousine to pick me up.

Dane: Where would she take you?

Maurice: She was involved in a rich women's club in the Miami area.

Dane: Did she give you gifts?

Maurice: Always. Watches, clothing. She would take me shopping and say, "Pick what you want." She would take me on trips, like a cruise, for a couple of weeks.

Toni: What did she tell her husband while she was on the cruise?

Maurice: Good question!

Toni: Did he know about your affair?

Maurice: I think he knew but didn't care. Probably had his own women.

Dane: How did the affair end?

Maurice: I ended it. She fell in love and pleaded with me, "Don't leave me, don't leave me." And she offered to give me anything I wanted, an apartment, a car, whatever it would take if I would just stay with her. And then I knew it was time to leave.

Dane: Did you feel bad about leaving her?

Maurice: Yes. I was sad for her.

Toni: Have you ever formed an emotional attachment with a client?

Maurice: Oh, you always get attached some. I am not a machine, you know. I can let myself care a little, but not a lot. I deserve to get my money, and then say good-bye. That's why I do this, after all.

Dane: Have you ever been in love?

Maurice: Yes, that's why I stopped doing this for a while. Because I was in love with a girl and wanted to have a normal life.

Toni: Did your girlfriend know about your past?

Maurice: I wasn't completely honest with her, and when I finally told her, she couldn't understand. She left. Shortly after that, a millionaire woman that I used to see for business called me and asked if I was ready to come back to her. I said yes.

Dane: Tell us about the third woman.

Maurice: It was more professional. Business-like. She was a — how do you say ? — dominatrix.

Toni: How did you feel about that?

Maurice: I don't mind. She wants to be the dominant one, fine. She wants to be on top, fine. And she wanted to play some games.

Dane: What kind of games?

Maurice: Slave and master.

Dane: Did she want to do that every time?

Maurice: Yes, at the end.

Dane: Did that cost more?

Maurice: Yes, yes. I'd make three or four thousand on these weekends.

Toni: Where did these sessions take place?

Maurice: At her friend's house.

Toni: Did her friend join in?

Maurice: It happened once. I was the master and they were the slaves. It was a classic game, and I love the classics! It took place in a beautiful home, white leather furniture, white marble floors, and a white canopy bed. I tied them both up with silk scarves, had them get on their knees, then I blindfolded them and had them pleasure me.

Later I dressed up as a priest, and they wanted to confess to me all of their sins. To absolve them, I had to whip them, and while one was being whipped, the other would chant softly in the background. After their confessions, I told them to worship my body. They enjoyed it; I enjoyed it. It was one of the most sensual experiences I've ever had.

Toni: What did you like least about being an escort?

Maurice: Collecting the money. Sometimes I was uncomfortable with that.

Toni: What about accepting gifts? Did that make you uncomfortable too?

Maurice: No. I was making gifts to them, too. You have to be a gentleman.

Dane: Do you plan to leave the business?

Maurice: No. I am still young, thirty-six, and in this country you can make good money doing this if you are French.

Toni: What do you think is the reason most of these women cheat on their husbands?

Maurice: Boredom. After being with the same man for thirty years, they want to try something new. They want excitement.

Dane: How important are looks in being a good male escort?

Maurice: You have to have personality and charm, above anything else. But looks are important, too. They pay for the package, and they don't pay for someone who is short, bald or fat.

Toni: Where do you see yourself in ten years?

Maurice: Still doing this.

Toni: How do you feel you've changed in your years of being an escort?

Maurice: Well, in the past if a woman offered me an apartment, I wouldn't take it. I always said no. But now, I'd take it.

Dane: What advice do you have for men who want to become escorts?

Maurice: To be a gentleman, have good manners and education. To be well-versed on a variety of topics, know a little bit about everything. And finally, to be a good listener. That is the key to the success.

Toni: Would you classify yourself as an escort or a gigolo?

Maurice: A gigolo lives off a woman. Everything paid for by the woman: the food, the car, trips, everything. Now you are a gigolo.

Toni: What's the difference?

Maurice: A gigolo is with the same woman. An escort is with different ladies, night after night. You earn your money. I was something in between.

Dane: What do you like best about American women?

Maurice: I like their liberated way.

Dane: What do you like least about them?

Maurice: They are not as romantic as the European women. They ask you right away, what kind of car do you drive, what kind of job do you have?

But I love all women, the European, the American. That's why I do this. I love the life and I enjoy the women.

World War II and the post-war years

On December 7, 1941, America entered World War II. As the nation marshalled every able-bodied citizen to support the war effort, six million women went to work. The number of women in the workforce swelled by 50 percent compared to pre-war years. Some earned good paychecks; women in defense manufacturing jobs averaged 40 percent higher pay than those in civilian jobs. The stereotype of women as "the weaker sex" vanished overnight and in its place Rosie the Riviter became a symbol of women's ability to do the job of any man.

World War II ended in a frenzy of patriotic jubilation with ticker tape parades for returning war heroes in every big city. As veterans went back to their jobs, women once again took up their role as homemakers. Manufacturing turned from tanks and planes to lawn mowers, toasters, vacuum cleaners, mixers and washing machines. Nest feathering became the national pastime. The birth rate shot up producing the generation of adults who today are known as "the baby boomers."

In the post-war period the image of women as wife, mother and homemaker was glorified on every front. Television shows such as *Ozzie and Harriet, Leave It To Beaver* and *Father Knows Best* [!] depicted scenes of beatific domesticity. Advertising campaigns featured housewives applying floor wax under the admiring gaze of their husbands, washing dishes that were so sparkling the neighbors were impressed, gushing over the features of the latest model refrigerator or the softness of a particular brand of toilet paper. Miss America was adulated for her qualities of mindless femininity and Mrs. America for her homemaking skills. Hominess was next to godliness. If a woman went to work, it was seen as a sign that her husband wasn't a good provider.

Still, women did go to work in increasing numbers. Salary aside, many housewives sought jobs just to break the monotony of a role that had begun to feel more like a prison than a blessing. In the 20-year period from the end of World War II the number of working women nearly doubled — from 13 million to 23 million.

The post-war boom led to the creation an unprecedented number of new jobs. The memory of Rosie the Riveter faded, however, and a decade later the message in the workplace was clear: Men get preferential treatment. The gains that women had made during the war years eroded. By 1965 women's earnings had slipped from 64 percent in of men's in 1951 to 60 percent. Women were routinely paid less than men for doing the exact same job.

After nearly two decades of struggling against gender stereotyping and bias in the workplace, something snapped. In 1963, *The Feminine Mystique* by Betty Friedan burst upon the scene. An immediate sensation, the book gave a whole generation of women words to express their pent-up frustrations. Friedan soon after helped to found the National Organization for Women (NOW) with a mission to "bring women into full participation in the mainstream of American society now, exercising all the privileges and responsibilities thereof in truly equal partnership with men."

Also in 1963, the birth control pill was approved for distribution and met with wide and immediate acceptance. Ten years later Roe v. Wade legalized abortion. These two events, for the first time in history, separated destiny from biology by giving women power over their own reproductive capacity. It also gave men the opportunity to sow their wild oats without fear of unwanted sprouts. Pleasure and procreation, too, were split asunder.

Well into the twentieth century, women's sexuality was defined by men in men's terms. The most influential thinker on the subject was Sigmund Freud. His contention that clitoral sexuality was an indication of immaturity and that fully adult women transferred sexual response from the clitoris to the vagina was widely accepted. In other words, "normal" for women was what worked best for satisfying a man.

Havelock Ellis and Alfred Kinsey challenged many of Freud's ideas, however it was not until 1966 when Masters and Johnson's book *Human Sexual Response* became a bestseller that Freud as king of the sexual theorists was dethroned. Their studies dealt a death blow to whatever was left of Freud's view of women as incomplete, inferior creatures pining away with penis envy. Masters and Johnson declared the clitoris to be as fully capable of pleasure as a man's penis. In fact, their work indicated that women were capable of an infinite variety of response patterns while men were capable of only one, making women the sexually superior gender. Americans of both genders leapt at the chance to test this proposition.

Enter, with a vengeance, the Sexual Revolution complete with premarital sex, extra-marital sex, recreational sex, anonymous sex, sex toys, sex-enhancing drugs, open marriage, one-night-stands, free love, group gropes, communes, mimi skirts, hot pants, and see-through blouses. Living together became a socially acceptable thing to do. The percentage of unmarried couples tripled between 1970 and 1980.

The high priest of the movement was Hugh Hefner, the shrewd and articulate founder of *Playboy* magazine and a network, in 1971 of twenty three Playboy Clubs and resorts.

Sexual liberation as it was touted by Hefner and practiced in the sixties and seventies ridiculed the Doris Day, goody two-shoes, "No,no, I'm not that kind of girl" model. The new sexually liberated woman was typified by the satin-eared, cotton-tailed Playboy Bunny whose form came as close as humanly possible to the immensely popular Barbie Doll.

Throughout the seventies, women defined women's sexuality with books that made the best seller lists. Germaine Greer's raunchy celebration of women's sexuality, *The Female Eunuch,* came out in 1970. Nancy Friday's collection of women's erotic fantasies, *My Secret Garden,* appeared in 1973. *The Hite Report,* by Shere Hite, contained interviews with "3,000 women, age 14 to 78, [who] describe in their own words their most intimate feelings about sex including: what they like — and don't like, how orgasm really feels — with and without intercourse... the importance of clitoral stimulation and masturbation." Scores of other books, by women, for women, about women, hit the bookstores in a torrent that continues today.

While Americans were screwing their brains out, the fabric of society was unraveling apace. The assassination of President Kennedy marked the end of Camelot and the beginning of a dark and torturous period in American history. More assassinations followed — Robert Kennedy, Martin Luther King, Malcolm X. As the war in Viet Nam escalated to nightmare proportions a civil war almost began at home. Four protesting college students were gunned down by National Guardsmen at Kent State. The Watergate scandal and then the resignation of President Nixon followed. Pleasure, by now, was not without a price. By the end of the seventies, even before the arrival of AIDS, sexually transmitted diseases (STDs) were tarnishing the Sexual Revolution. The taking of American hostages in Iran led to a humbling of the next American president, Jimmy Carter, by a mad monk on the other side of the world. Even during the economic boom of the eighties, the Senate's Iran-Contra hearings raised searing questions about the credibility of President Ronald Reagan. And a deep and intractable economic recession clouded the end of the Bush administration. Political disillusionment characterized the American mood for nearly three decades.

The innocent, free-spirited, optimistic days of the flapper and her gigolo seemed a millennium away.

Mitch

TONI's note: I felt extremely uncomfortable during this interview. Mitch's attitudes toward women were at times so offensive I wanted to end the discussion. However, because Dane and I wanted a representative sampling of escort personalities, we decided to include his interview in the book.

A contact we made in a Ft. Lauderdale nightclub referred us to Mitch. We met at the rooftop pool of an oceanside hotel. He was blond, 5 feet 10 inches, 175 pounds of Italian bravado.

Up to this point, I had thought male escorts liked women, probably a little too much in order to be in this line of work. From Mitch, I learned that a male escort can actually hate women while making love to them.

He linked sex to physical force, using such phrases as: "show the woman who's boss," "they wanna be attacked," "I owned it by taking it from her," and "women want to be dominated." Not unlike a rapist, he seemed to feel that women want violence. At times he would jump out of his chair, wave his fists in the air to illustrate a point, and then pound the table. He resembled a wild animal, dangerous and unpredictable, anger barely leashed.

Dane: What was your most successful line with women?

Mitch: Oh, I have lots of 'em. But I think the best was one time at a bar. This great looking group of girls were standing around. All these guys were just hanging over them, trying to talk to them, and I just walked up to the girls and said, "Hey. You want to go get high with a serial killer?" And they thought it was pretty funny. Ended up going home with me. All four of them.

Toni: What do you think is the secret to being a successful male escort?

Mitch: Well, it's not that you go out and it's a job and you hustle. The real insight is finding the beautiful woman, like you, Toni, and one who's wealthy. Because you have an ego, Toni, whether you think you do or not. You're more susceptible to the con than an ugly woman.

Toni: And why is that, Mitch?

Mitch: Because an ugly girl knows what she's worth. They know they're going to have to pay for it, for sex, and that's it.

Toni: Do you really believe that?

Mitch: Definitely. And if the con is done right, she enjoys it while she's gettin' it. Oh, man, you can really con a beautiful woman if you do it right.

Toni: I see.

Mitch: Am I making you mad, Toni?

Toni: Not at all. I find it interesting how you relate to a woman. Flattery and insults in the same breath. Has this approach really worked for you?

Mitch: (laughs) All the time, babe. You don't get anywhere if you're a nice guy.

Dane: Do you believe women want a guy who treats them bad?

Mitch: Absolutely. But the trick is, you don't do it all the time. Look, I think you have to show the woman who's in charge the first night. You have to take her sexually. After that you treat 'em loving. But you have to step over that line with her the first time. A beautiful woman is used to calling the shots: "Jump." "How high?" They wanna be attacked more than any other woman.

Toni: So you look at the whole thing as a game? A con? With women as the marks?

Mitch: It's not so much a con as finding the right prey.

Dane: Mitch, tell us about your hobbies.

Mitch: Sure. I'm writing my memoirs, and I just happen to have the beginning paragraph right here. OK, it's called "King of Beasts." Question: What is the most intelligent, cunning, ruthless animal on earth? Answer: The beautiful, young woman who is married to the rich, older man. Whether this woman has come from a wealthy family or married her way into one, you can bet that she is a predator by nature, heartbreaker by choice, and knows that she literally has the world by the balls.

That was based on an experience that happened to me right here on the beach in Ft. Lauderdale.

Dane: Tell us about it.

Mitch: It was the perfect con. I was lying on the sand reading a book when this gorgeous girl came walking up the beach. All the other guys were using their best lines to pick her up. I just lay there and watched, laughing inside, because I saw her starting to look bored. Well, she got tired of those idiots and walked away from them.

I saw her looking at me. Probably because I was ignoring her. She was curious and I was making her come to me. I knew I had her then.

She said, "Nice day," or something, and told me her name was

Brittany. Anyway, we started getting along. I noticed this diamond ring she had. Gigantic! She told me her husband was a very wealthy older man who owns several TV stations in Australia.

During the conversation, she asked, "What do you do beside read books on the beach?" I stared right into those baby blues and said, "I find beautiful young women who are married to rich, older men. Then give them what they need and take what I want in return."

She looked stunned. Inside, I was loving every minute of it. I told her I was just joking, and that I had to be getting to work. She didn't want me to go. I had her figured out. She was a spoiled brat, used to getting what she wants, and now she wanted me.

I told her if I'd stay, I'd lose my job. I said I had bills to pay. She asked how much I owed and I said, "Eleven hundred dollars." The dollar figure is very important, not too high, not too low. Besides, eleven is my lucky number.

All of a sudden she said, "Will traveler's checks do?"

Politely, I refused, saying, "I have a lot of pride."

She said, "It won't be a handout if you can be my tour guide while I'm in Ft. Lauderdale." Then she said she'd pay what I need and more.

You see, girls like her are used to getting what they want. They love challenges, like stealing another woman's man. So I played that angle.

I told her I had a girlfriend and how much in love I was, that I thought she was beautiful and I was oh, so tempted, but I just couldn't hurt my girlfriend.

So Brittany says, "Look, Mitch. You're already cheating on her in your mind. So why don't you go all the way?"

She kissed me and invited me to dinner, saying, "It's all settled." Then she took me shopping and bought me some clothes. We spent about a grand. Had a lot of fun. She was a nice girl, in a way.

That evening at dinner, she gave me a check for two thousand dollars, enough to cover my bills and a little extra for being a tour guide. And she gave me a room key. I had this incredible feeling of power.

After dinner we took the elevator to her penthouse suite. In between floors I pushed the stop button. I knew she wanted it, and I was going to take it my way. I lifted up her skirt and did her right there in the elevator. She loved it. She wanted more.

I took her into the room and told her to strip and lick the sweat off my body. I played with her, told her what a bad girl she was, tied her up and spanked her.

Then I hauled her into the shower and cooled her off. I bent her over the sink, grabbed her hair and pulled her face up so she could see us both, and I took her again. She changed her tune. Instead of begging me for more, she was begging me to stop.

I tucked her in bed, kissed her goodnight, and went through her purse. I took some cash, maybe five hundred bucks or so, and went to leave.

She never asked about the five hundred bucks (I doubt she even noticed it was gone), and called the next day. For the next two weeks I had an incredible time. Had great sex and got paid almost ten thousand dollars, not including jewelry and other cash I stole.

Then she took me to Vegas for the weekend. We gambled, and then it was over. When she had to leave, she left. I never saw her again. But I gave her jewelry to the next wealthy woman I saw on the beach. And that's kind of how it all started.

Toni: Do you think sex is about control?

Mitch: Of course! I think with Brittany because I had the audacity to just take control of the situation, and the fact that she thought she was in control turned her on. I made her do everything I wanted her to do. She was mine. Her husband damn well never did that, and I'm sure none of the boys at school did that.

Dane: How old was she?

Mitch: She was only twenty-one, married to a fifty-two-year-old man.

Toni: What if the woman you were with was less than attractive?

Mitch: I wouldn't be with her. That's what I never understood about these other male escorts. I mean, how can you get your psyche up to do an ugly woman? You just can't. You gotta want to.

Dane: Do you always give them that story about having a girlfriend?

Mitch: Always. I say, "I've got a girlfriend, and I love her. But as I'm lying in bed here with you this evening, I could be with another woman tomorrow. That's not your fault. It's mine. The way it was so intimate and beautiful with you tonight, it could be that way with another woman tomorrow." I don't know why. I just thank God for it.

I told every woman I was with I had a girlfriend. And they'd always say, "If you're so happy with her, what are you doing in bed with me?" And they'd eat it up. They'd give me more, better sex. They'd do more for me. They wanted to be my girlfriend, but I wouldn't even spend the night.

Real playboys never spend the night.

Same thing with calling girls back. You make 'em wait for it. I didn't call this one girl back for a week once, and she was all over me like a hornet. And I owned her by taking it from her, too.

Dane: What about charging for a date? How is that done?

Mitch: A good escort doesn't have to charge. You get what you're worth. You get her car, her credit card, take her pocket money, her jewelry. Tell her to go get more. It's brutal, but it's the way it works. At least with me. It's all in the attitude, you know?

Women look at me and say, "Wow, nothing scares him," and that turns them on. And it scares all the men.

Dane: Do you think other men are threatened by you?

Mitch: Definitely. As soon as I walk into a nightclub, I smell it. I feel it. I see them hold on to their girlfriends tighter. I look guys right in the eye. They're bold enough to look at me, I look at their woman. I look at her, that's right, I looked at your fucking woman, so what?

Dane: What was your childhood like?

Mitch: Oh, I used to get beat as a kid because girls would look at me, and their guys wouldn't like it. In fact, when I was in the Navy I heard there was a guy who put a bounty on me to wreck my face, so much money by midnight if someone could disfigure me. Happened in Perth, Australia.

If I wanted to, sure, I could be meekish and not look at the girls, but I'm on the prowl and I want to be a predator. A lot of guys are like that, and I can tell the players from the non-players. One, two, three, I can tell you the guys that are gonna get laid, and those that ain't. You can see it in their eyes.

And I never let my ego get too big when I went home with a beautiful woman. I checked behind doors. I'd go in the bathrooms. I make sure everything is safe.

One time one summer a sailor got three women. They tied him up, a meek kind of guy, wasn't tough. He was found three days later, tied to a bed, a big fucking vibrator stuck up his butt. Man! He had a section 8, went crazy. He just wasn't the same after that.

Toni: It doesn't sound as though you think women can be trusted.

Mitch: You can never trust women. The only woman you can trust is your mother.

That sailor incident happened in Australia. The Australian women, they wanna get it over there so bad, it's crazy. Anybody can get laid in Australia.

Dane: Do you think men are more faithful or women?

Mitch: Women. See, a man can say he's faithful because nobody put no pussy in his face. I think men are faithful by default. Women, they turn it down.

Dane: Have you ever been faithful?

Mitch: Sure. I was faithful for two years once. But then I met this other girl, a regional manager for a large corporation. She was young, beautiful, rich and had that look in her eye. I had a joint in my ashtray and we were driving somewhere, and I asked her, "What are your vices?" I was feeling her out a bit, you know. "Do you drink?"

She says, "No."

"Do you do drugs?"

"No."

"Gambling?"

"No."

"Well, then, what do you do? What's your vice?"

She says, "Sex."

So there, predator by default, right out the window. I unbuttoned the shirt, unbuttoned the pants. It happened. I was unfaithful the first moment of opportunity. That's when I knew I was right for this line of work.

And one other thing. Maybe it sounds like I'm justifying being lazy, because I get everything paid for. But I wonder, is lazy so bad?

Dane: Tell us about your experiences in the Navy.

Mitch: I was seventeen when I first got in the Navy. An older personnel clerk checked me in. He was gay. He said that I was good-looking, that I should get out there and meet some women. And I said I had no money. They guy said, "You got fifty cents? Take the bus. A quarter to the beach and a quarter to get back in case you don't get lucky. And you go to one of the rich hotels on the beach. Get a towel, lay out, and you wait. Don't say anything. Just wait. Some beautiful woman will approach you. The ugly ones won't because they know they're outta their league. But the real vain ones, the ones that get hit on all day... You sit there and she's gonna wonder whether you're a fag or what. You got her then."

Toni: Sounds like he helped to form your impressions of women.

Mitch: Oh, he clued me in to the psyche of women: that women are most vicious to other women, that men couldn't cheat if other women didn't let them. I mean, if there's a cheating problem, it's not because of men. It's because of women. If women stuck together like a sisterhood, and they didn't fuck another woman's man, it would be a different story.

Anyway, so we're in Sidney, Australia. One time I come back to the ship late. They all hate me, mostly the officers because I'm getting laid more than they are. But I was a pirate and I had these girls lined up on the beach. Anyway, so that night I get brought back to the ship in a Jaguar, and I was a whole ten minutes late and right away they said, "Take his fucking I. D. card; he's restricted."

I'm like, "Screw you, I had a good time. We're leaving in two days anyway."

This woman I had been with calls up the ship and says, "Well, am I gonna see you tonight?"

I say, "Nah, they took my I. D. card."

She laughs, "That's gonna stop you? You're only gonna be here once in your life. I have this hotel room on the beach, and you're gonna stay on the ship?"

And I'm like, "No, I ain't. I'll think of something." And I did.

I knew you could get off the ship to go jog on the pier. She happened to be a doctor. So, I was found passed out jogging at the end of the pier. She was driving by. I had no I.D. card on me, so they couldn't identify me until I'd wake up. She rescued me. I even got a letter from her hospital, sealed and signed and everything.

They had to search for me, man. That night nobody could find me anywhere. I was off- coast with her.

When I came back the next day they had me in irons. The Captain was bullshit. He took the letter, then laughed all the way to his quarters.

The Captain was a pirate, too. He screwed two girls at a time once. And one night when he was with a girl, and she took a fancy to me, and I thought: "Oh, oh. Trouble." I said, "Captain, I'll leave the club. No problem." But he says, "Hey, there's enough in here for everyone. She wants you, go with her." The Captain was real cool.

Dane: Have you ever deliberately gone after a friend's girl?

Mitch: I didn't have to. They kept 'em away from me. Couples that used to swing wouldn't let their girl fuck me because I was so arrogant and they knew I'd fuck the shit out of them, and they'd like it too much.

Toni: You really believe that?

Mitch: Toni, I'm trying to be humble, but the things I find important in life are: fighting, fucking, and gambling. And fucking is how I kept a woman.

Dane: Did you ever fear a man taking your girl?

Mitch: What, are you kidding? It would never happen because I give a girl too much. I give 'em what they always wanted: hard on the outside, soft on the inside. Women want the combination. I can be sensual for a long time, tease her, kiss and caress, and tell her, "I'm gonna touch you everywhere except those places." Until it just boils, man. You fuck her so hard she's hurt, until she can't take no more. You give her what she wants.

Once in awhile you make love to her real nice, so they can see the soft side of you. I think a woman will never leave a man if he shows his true sensual side.

I think every woman wants to be pushed over the line. You gotta teasingly give it and take it away at the same time.

Dane: Have you ever been with two girls at once?

Mitch: Yeah, I fucked two sisters right in the men's bathroom in a night-club once. My friend made sure nobody came in. And then when he finally left and a guy came in, he's like, "Hey, man, you got girls in the men's room."

And I said, "Hey, what's the matter with you, can't you see I'm getting laid in here or what?" The two sisters, they did each other, they did me, they did my friend.

Dane: How do you classify yourself, Mitch?

Mitch: As a real American gangster. An outlaw. It's up to you to find the opportunity and grab it. By not working, I've supported my lifestyle over these years. I make my living from women. I'm kind of a gangster of love.

You take what you want in this world. You take from women because it is the natural order of things. Women want to be dominated. They want to know that the man is in charge. Most men ain't doing it right. You know, it's not like: "Oh, honey, we need to have a discussion." And she says, "Not now, I'm busy."

A real man says, "Bitch, sit your fucking ass down and you're gonna listen to what the fuck I got to say!"

Dane: Let's talk about blackmailing. Do escorts ever try to set up their clients?

Mitch: Some guys are into blackmailing by videotaping their clients. I'm not. But this is how it works: you set up a secret videotape and film the whole night. Then you follow them home and find out their address. Then you come back when no one's home and get the husband's name off the mail. Then you show the lady a copy of the tape, and say, "This is what it's gonna cost you."

And while you're taking their money, jewelry, credit cards or whatever, you're laughing the whole time because what's she gonna do? Complain to her husband? Call the cops? You got her. That's how you use the con with women. The only problem is guys who do this stuff tend to disappear.

Dane: Where's the best place to meet wealthy women in Florida?

Mitch: The best scene is Palm Beach and Boca Raton, in the best hotels on the beaches. There's a lot of wealthy, lonely women out there just looking for guys like me. I have great success there.

Toni: One last question. What's the most expensive gift a woman's ever given you?

Mitch: Her friends.

Cassandra

Dane interviewed Cassandra over the phone one evening. She was referred by one of her escorts. She was quite guarded about what she would reveal about herself. What was striking about her was that her attitude toward her experiences with escorts was so similar to the way men traditionally see their encounters with prostitutes. To her, the escorts were just bodies with nameless faces who performed a service for pay – no involvement, no feelings, just sex.

Dane: What name would you like to use for this interview?

Cassandra: Let's use Cassandra.

Dane: What's your profession, Cassandra?

Cassandra: I'm a corporate lawyer. I'm constantly surrounded by men because of being a lawyer. They're always coming on to me, trying to impress me with what they have rather than what they are.

Dane: Where do you originally come from?

Cassandra: Actually, I'm from South Carolina.

Dane: Have you ever been married?

Cassandra: Oh, yes. Twice. And I must admit both divorces left me very well off.

Dane: You must be very beautiful to have all these men come on to you. Can you give me a description of yourself?

Cassandra: I'm thirty-eight. I've got long, dark, flowing hair, green eyes. I guess I'm about 5 foot 8 in my stocking feet and 125 pounds. I don't think I'm too bad to look at. I have been offered jobs as a model, but I've never really had the time or the interest.

Dane: Why do you pay for sex?

Cassandra: This could get kind of involved. I don't really want any commitment. I guess that is why both of my marriages failed. I was fooling around even then.

Dane: You were a naughty girl.

Cassandra: I like what I like, and if I pay for it, I get what I like.

Dane: What sexual preferences do you have?

Cassandra: Well, I like being tied up, and my favorite is to have two or more doing everything at the same time. Actually I like cheap motels too. The sleazier the better.

Dane: How do you get these men?

Cassandra: I use an escort service. Or services, I should say. One just isn't really enough.

Dane: How come, Cassandra?

Cassandra: Well, variety is the spice of life, don't you think?
And the escort services tend to screen their staff to where I feel a bit safer. I'd never pick anyone up off the street. Heavens, you never know what you might get.

Dane: How do you contact these escorts?

Cassandra: Well, I use my beeper to contact them. And I leave my voice mail number under another name, of course. Being a high profile lawyer, I can't possibly let the public know what I'm doing.

Dane: Do you change your appearance?

Cassandra: Sometimes I wear a wig. Sometimes I wear glasses. Little things.

Dane: What's the most bizarre, kinky experience you've ever had?

Cassandra: There's nothing really exotic. There's been a couple of times that scared me because I wasn't quite cautious enough.

Dane: Can you tell me about one of those incidents?

Cassandra: No.

Dane: How do you protect yourself against any violence? How do you screen these guys?

Cassandra: As I said, I use the different services, and some of them take a bit more time making sure they have good escorts.

Dane: Tell me about one of your sexual encounters.

Cassandra: One time I requested two muscular gentlemen to come and meet me in the parking lot of a restaurant. The scenario was that my car was broke down, and, of course, these two gorgeous hunks, being the gentlemen that they were, came to the aid of a lady. I was dressed to the hilt, wearing a mini skirt and fishnet stockings and four-inch heels. I had my hair down, and it was a bit windy so it was blowing around. And a nice, big V-neck blouse that showed plenty of cleavage.

Dane: How much did you pay each of these guys and how did you act out the scene?

Cassandra: They were paid quite generously, I believe — five hundred dollars apiece. The scene basically was for them to usher me into their vehicle to take me to a garage to see about getting some service for my car. But on the way to the garage we tended to get sidetracked, went up into a nice, little secluded area..

Dane: Like a little one-act play.

Cassandra: Oh, it was more than one act.

Dane: What makes you get into that kind of sexual scene?

Cassandra: Men have always been so domineering, and they all seem to think with their dicks. They don't know enough to think with their minds. And I'm more than just another pussy. I've got a brain as well. I guess this is my way of getting even because I control the show.

Dane: What is your frame of mind now?

Cassandra: I feel like there is more than one person in this body. Sometimes I'm a very little girl who is very vulnerable. Other times I'm this powerful witch... or bitch.

Dane: Are you seeing a therapist?

Cassandra: Oh, yes. I have been for about three years now. I don't think she really completely understands me, or at least that's how I perceive it.

Dane: Are your problems too complex for her? Too deep?

Cassandra: Unless you've walked a mile in my shoes, you're not really going to understand how I feel or how I think.

Dane: It sounds to me like you have these fantasies and these urges and, all of a sudden, they come to a head and you act on them. You make that phone call.

Cassandra: That's about the size of it. When I can't handle it myself, I call in the troops.

Dane: How much money do you make in your profession, being a lawyer?

Cassandra: I'm in the one hundred thousand range.

Dane: Do you know how much you've spent on these escorts these last three years?

Cassandra: I've never really kept track of it. I know it was worth every penny, though.

Dane: Escort doesn't seem to be the proper terminology in your case. What else would you call them?

Cassandra: They're bodies with nameless faces. They perform a service for which I pay, and then I forget them.

Dane: Did you ever see the same one twice?

Cassandra: On occasion, but rarely. I like variety.

Dane: Are you going to keep on doing this?

Cassandra: That's a good question. I guess I'll have to find out the answer from my next shrink.

Dane: How often do you have these urges?

Cassandra: I have to make a call about once a month, every once in a while twice a month.

Dane: What advice would you have for any women considering paying for sex, for companionship or, as in your case, for fulfilling fantasies?

Cassandra: To start with, don't condemn it until you've tried it. If you've got the money, give it a go. You might find you like it.

Ryan

At a diner in West Ft. Lauderdale, we sat down with Ryan and were convinced we had met Dr. Jekyll and Mr. Hyde incarnate. Referred to us by a counselor, he seemed to be two people, a caring, sensitive person one minute, then a tough, callous person who spoke matter-of-factly about violence the next. Perhaps he appeals to women with a desire to walk on the edge.

Ryan is 5 feet 11 inches, 165 pounds with thinning, brown hair, an engaging grin and bedroom eyes.

Toni: When did you get started in this business?

Ryan: In 1986. I was going to school at night and working days. I just wanted some extra money and I needed a second job, one that paid decently and was worth my time to do it. So that was my motivation, being a student and working. I liked dating and I was doing drugs, some coke, grass, it all required money. And then I saw an ad in the paper.

Toni: For escorts?

Ryan: Yes.

Toni: What did the ad say? Do you remember?

Ryan: I think it said something like, "Companion wanted," I forget the exact wording. But I pretty much knew what it meant.

Dane: So what happened when you called up this ad?

Ryan: The guy said to come on in. When I went in, he basically just wanted to see what my dick looked like.

Toni: Are you serious?

Ryan: Yes. That is what he wanted and you could tell that he liked it.

Dane: He wanted to see it physically?

Ryan: Yeah. He wanted to touch it, too. He liked what he saw. I mean, he put on some porno movies so I could get an erection. He really enjoyed measuring me. He was real happy because the thing came out like 9 1/2 inches, or something. Anyway, he was delighted. To me it was just my dick. No thing of beauty.

He was Italian and from Boston. I'm Italian and originally from Boston too. So we got along on a superficial level. But I could tell he was definitely into more. I also can be somewhat manipulative, so if he wanted to give me joints and measure my dick, so be it. In terms of ego, it was nice.

Toni: Did you make it clear that you wanted to be with women?

Ryan: Oh, yeah. He wanted me to do men. And he wanted me to do him.

I think what ended up happening was he wasn't sending me out much on jobs because he wanted me for himself. I think he was hoping that I'd change my mind. I only did men once or twice.

Dane: So he set up the arrangements for you?

Ryan: Yeah. It was set up so I would check in periodically or he would call me. The deal was that he would tell me what they were like. If I thought it sounded like something that I wanted to do, I gave him the OK. I'd have him give them my phone number. Then they'd call and I'd talk to them and make arrangements from there.

Dane: When do you collect the money?

Ryan: The minute you get in the door, you are supposed to collect the money and call the office. I mean, this is the first thing before any sex happens.

After you've been in the business awhile, you can kind of gauge how much time to spend doing small talk, collecting money, and all the stuff. Then you kind of develop a plan of how long you are going to stay or whatever. So if you were gone too long, the office would send someone out to check on you. Make sure everything was OK.

Toni: How much money did you normally make per hour?

Ryan: Two hundred and fifty dollars for an hour, and the agency took forty percent.

Dane: What were the women like that you were with?

Ryan: All kinds. Older, usually. Some were attractive. Some were not. Anyway, I did it for about a year, and then I just got a bad feeling about it.

Toni: Can you tell us what that bad feeling was?

Gigolos · **125**

Ryan: The bad feeling was that, even though from a sociological perspective I was a gigolo or stud, I was basically a whore. So in my heart, that's how I felt about myself. I was a whore.

Dane: What was the difference between female clients and male clients?

Ryan: Well, I only did men a couple of times. But, I guess the thing is women won't screw you around like a man would. A man would get off on making you do degrading things. A woman isn't that way. So there is a certain amount of safety there. And a woman will usually treat you pretty good.

I mean, when you walk in the door, she's not going to tell you to get on your knees and degrade you about what she wants done to her. But a man would probably make you do things like that just for the hell of it.

There was one guy I was with that I had a bad feeling about. I was worried that this guy might be connected with the Mob. There was just something about him. I have relatives up north and I know how that shit works. They got their hands in it, especially down here in Ft. Lauderdale.

Toni: What gave you the impression that he was connected with the Mob?

Ryan: Just because he was Italian. I got ten uncles. I know how it works. If you have to get in touch with "The Man," and you're Italian and from the Northeast, you can.

Toni: Do you think the Mob is involved with the escort business?

Ryan: Yes. It has its hands in everything just about, especially down here. This is where they all go to hang out. And there's an old adage: This is where mobsters retire.

Dane: What areas of Ft. Lauderdale are operated or influenced by the Mob?

Ryan: Oh, lots of places. Like, I once had a landscaping company down here and did a job for this one guy. He had a big hotel. That is where he hides his money and shit. He was from New Jersey.

I mean, this guy wasn't just connected. He was it. He was "The Man." I think he was a capo. And what happened was, at the end of the night, he basically didn't pay us. He decided he wasn't paying and that was it. And you don't argue with these guys.

Dane: You said you've serviced women. And you've serviced men. Have you ever been with a couple?

Ryan: Yeah. My first referral was a husband and wife. He told me he wanted me to do his wife while he watched. I said, "That's fine with me." They had a beautiful place in Emerald Hills, very impressive.

I met them at the door. He was kind of a fat, middle-aged guy with a cigar. And she was the same except she didn't have a cigar.

Anyhow, I remember catching a glimpse of him putting the kids to bed, and that just kind of turned my stomach. I immediately developed a distaste for these people. It might have been judgmental on my part, but, still, it made the process easier for me. I mean, I really felt uncomfortable with the kids there. It just didn't seem right. I tried to put it out of my mind and just get down to business.

Dane: What did they want you to do?

Ryan: Basically what it entailed was me abusing his wife while he watched. It made it easier because I didn't have much respect for them anyway. I wanted to punish them in a way; I didn't like them.

Toni: How did he want you to abuse his wife?

Ryan: Call her every name in the book. He left it up to me. I slapped her around a bit, but not too much. I really wasn't into that. I mean, it's one thing to play at it, but another thing to actually, physically hurt someone. You can tie someone up and have fun and play out a fantasy, but to hurt someone, that is crossing the line. I don't normally play that.

Toni: What was her attitude about you slapping her and calling her names?

Ryan: She loved it. The more I could do to her the more she wanted it. She just wanted me to treat her as badly as I could, call her terrible rotten things.

Toni: So you were calling her names and it was exciting you, and you were hitting her.

Ryan: A little bit. Yeah, I roughed her up. I didn't just let her get on her knees. I forced her to her knees.

Dane: What were you doing while you were hitting her?

Ryan: I made her suck me. I fucked her mouth. In that way I was very rough with her.

Toni: Did you feel a sense of power as you were doing this?

Ryan: It was power, definitely. It was a woman on her knees, so basically whatever I said, she did.

Actually I started ordering the husband around, too, the little piece of shit. He had this big fucking belly. He was just like a little Buddha.

Dane: What was he doing while you were doing his wife? Was he watching?

Ryan: He was doing coke and smoking a cigar.

Toni: But he was getting off by watching this?

Ryan: Yeah. I guess. I had a distaste for the whole thing.

Dane: You were enjoying it, but it was distasteful to you in another way, right?

Ryan: Because they were distasteful, it made me enjoy it. It was kind of weird.

Toni: Were you worried that you might like it too much, some of the stuff you were doing, like the hitting and the name calling?

Ryan: No. I know me pretty good by now. I stop right on the edge. But I have to see that edge to know. That is the way I am.

Dane: So you had the encounter with the Buddha and Mrs. Buddha.

Ryan: Yes.

Dane: What did she look like?

Ryan: Not all that great-looking, middle-aged, dumpy, glasses. Probably in her forties.

Dane: What kind of names did she like you to call her?

Ryan: "Cunt." She would get off on that and "dirty whore" and shit like that. I called her all kinds of names.

Toni: How did you feel when you were doing that?

Ryan: I liked it.

Dane: Did you really?

Ryan: Yes. I liked it a lot.

Toni: Why?

Ryan: Because I'm a little twisted. And then, when Mr. Buddha left the room, I started calling her more stuff. I said some disgusting things to her. Like, "I sat on your face, bitch, and you loved it" and stuff like that. She liked that.

Toni: Did you enjoy it more when the husband was watching or when he left the room?

Ryan: I liked it more when he left the room. I made her lick every inch of my body. I enjoyed doing that to her, dominating her.

Toni: Did you feel more free to do whatever you wanted with her when the husband left the room?

Ryan: After a while, I didn't care if he was there or not. At one point he joined in a bit. She loved it. At one point he got on the bed. I think I was giving her some head, and he made her give him some head. We were both kind of doing her.

Dane: What did they pay you for that?

Ryan: I was there maybe a couple of hours. I think I told them seven hundred and fifty dollars. And then this guy got all uptight and wasn't going to give me shit. The wife said, "He was good, pay the man. And give him a tip." I'll never forget that. The Budda gave me like eight hundred dollars cash.

Toni: Did you ever see this couple again?

Ryan: About ten days later they called. I went over there and we started in, and then the wife just flipped out.

Dane: What happened?

Ryan: She just didn't want to do it. I think I was giving her some head and she just flipped out. The last time she was telling me how good I was at it.

Dane: Maybe the thrill was gone.

Ryan: This time she just wasn't into it. She started pushing us away.

Dane: You and the husband?

Ryan: Yeah.

Dane: Do you know why?

Ryan: Yes. I think there was too much coke going on. Anyway, so I did some more coke. I took a joint too. I said, "Give me my damn money," and I left. I got another two hundred dollars out of them for like twenty minutes worth of work.

Toni: Ryan, you said she was pushing you both away.

Ryan: Yeah, yeah.

Toni: What was the husband doing at this point?

Ryan: Same type of thing as me. He was trying to make her suck him.

Toni: You mentioned that the wife was "dumpy" looking. Was it hard for you to be excited about someone that you didn't find appealing?

Ryan: No. I like women and I like sex. I try not to judge people too much on how they look. I'm not real rigid, which helps to make this job a little easier. Hey, we all look kind of funky with our clothes off. You might find two in a hundred that look like someone you might want to be with.

Dane: Was that the most bizarre experience you had?

Ryan: No. Once I met this woman at a trade show. She was a sales rep, dressed real nice, heels and a tight blue suit. I made a date with her for after the show. Gave her a phony name, of course, and followed her home.

Immediately, as soon as I walked in her door, I just like attacked her.

Toni: What do you mean "attacked?"

Ryan: I pulled a knife on her. She didn't even know me. And I wasn't getting paid for this. I was doing this for me. I couldn't control myself. You must think I'm crazy, huh?

Toni: A little twisted, maybe. So what did she do when you pulled the knife?

Ryan: What?

Toni: How did she feel? How did she react?

Ryan: Oh, yeah. Well, I said to her, "I met you at a trade show, so nobody even knows that I exist. Therefore, I could kill you right now and nobody would ever know."

Toni: Do you think that excited her?

Ryan: It scared the shit out of her. It excited me, though. I don't know why. I know that I couldn't have actually killed her.

Dane: Can you describe this woman a little more?

Ryan: Thin. Tall. Maybe forty-two, and nice-looking, but there was something about her, I could tell. She was a hippie. Grew up in San Francisco, a French Canadian. She had gone through a bad divorce.

Dane: How did the date end?

Ryan: I tied her up and scared the shit out of her. After a while it seemed she was getting off on this whole scene, so I untied her. We screwed our brains out for a few hours. I think I spent the night. Actually, it ended up very loving. It was wild.

I mean, I can be a prick, but at the same time, I'm not the type that runs out of bed. I have no problem with cuddling and spending the night and waking you up in the morning with a kiss.

Dane: You spent the night?

Ryan: Yes. She made me breakfast too.

Toni: She made you breakfast after you scared the shit out of her?

Ryan: She was a good woman.

Dane: I wonder what she would have done if you put a gun in her mouth?

Toni: Probably bought you a new wardrobe.

Ryan: Actually, Toni, she did take me to the store and buy me a new wardrobe. These are the pants she bought me.

Dane: Do you still see her?

Ryan: Yesterday, in fact, I had to order some more clothes and I called her and told her what I needed. I was hoping to get a little something for Christmas, but I guess not because she told me not to call her anymore.

Dane: She said don't call her?

Ryan: Right. I think she's seeing someone else.

Toni: She was paying you?

Ryan: Yeah. Some money and, of course, the clothes. This has been going on for the past two years.

Dane: How many times did you see her all together?

Ryan: Thirty, forty times.

Dane: How often during a week?

Ryan: Maybe twice a month.

Dane: Would it be an encounter like with the knife and that type of stuff?

Ryan: No. That was just that one time.

Toni: You have to have variety, right?

Ryan: Yes. I would come up with other things. One time we did a scene from a movie. Sometimes I wouldn't even tie her up. I would bend her over the couch and spank her. I would be pretty rough with her. Sometimes I would come over with flowers and be real sweet and comb her hair and love the shit out of her. It was all depending on my mood.

Toni: So it depended on your mood?

Ryan: Right.

Toni: Her mood didn't matter?

Ryan: Right. If she had a say in it, it wouldn't work.

Toni: Do you think women want to be dominated sexually?

Ryan: I can spot the ones that do. It's a feeling you get when you first meet them. You take a risk. Sometimes it pays off.

I find that most of the women I've been with have not been adverse to spanking. They seemed to enjoy it. There is also a way of doing it. The more you do it, the better you get at it. In other words, you don't just spring something like that on someone. There is a way to approach the matter. You don't just call them a whore and start slapping them around.

Dane: You get a routine down, so to speak?

Ryan: Exactly.

Toni: Have you had some serious relationships with girlfriends?

Ryan: Some, but I'm not too good at that. I don't know why. For a long time, I wanted to try and screw every woman in the world. I guess it's just the way I am.

Toni: Did being an escort seem kind of glamorous to you?

Ryan: I thought it was. But I knew I wasn't no American Gigolo. I was more like a Midnight Cowboy. Aside from all the taboo and the connotations surrounding the business, I halfway enjoyed it. I didn't grow a third eyeball or anything. I tried it, and then got out.

Toni: If you had the opportunity to get back into it again, would you take it?

Ryan: I might. Why, do you have somebody for me to call?

Toni: No, no.

Dane: The women that you were with, what do you think they weren't getting from their relationships that they needed you?

Ryan: Domination. At the same time, you don't have to abuse them in terms of making them feel worthless. You can actually make them feel very special. Like that movie, *9 1/2 Weeks*. In that movie, he put her on a pedestal. She was like an angel. He bought her everything she could desire as long as she played the game.

One day she stuck a pin in the balloon and saw that he was just a man. Actually, a pathetic man.

It was funny because I saw the movie with a bunch of people in the room and a lot of them were like women feminists and stuff, and they were going off. I just kind of sat in the back and thought he was real pathetic and that the movie was more about him than her. When she walked out on him, I could feel the way he felt. He was so surprised, he completely died. He was crushed.

Dane: Do you have regular clients that you see?

Ryan: Yeah, I see this one woman regularly. I've been friends with her for six years. She has other boyfriends, but every now and then we kind of look at each other and something happens. We tear each other up for forty-five minutes, and then, that's it. It might not happen for six or eight months or a year. We just go along being real good friends.

She is overweight, though. Very pretty, but overweight. Because of that, I never really thought of her seriously. But she's like my best friend.

She's got a kid, and sometimes I take her kid all day and bring him home at night. I've become like a surrogate father or something.

Toni: Any other relationships?

Ryan: Well, there was another girl. I almost wound up living with her. She moved into my apartment. We started unloading boxes. She was a Latin girl, real hot, real nice, from El Salvador.

Anyway, she had these little figurines. For some reason when she put them on the counter next to my telephone, I lost it. It was like no longer my apartment because I had feminine stuff around or something.

I literally started putting her stuff back in the boxes as she was unloading them. I don't even think I lasted two days with her moving in. I moved her out as fast as I moved her in because she took them damn figurines and put them on the counter.

Toni: Do you think you like to stay detached in relationships?

Ryan: Most definitely.

Dane: What was your family life like?

Ryan: My dad is like a stone. A slab of granite, and that's all he knows. He had a really hard, hard life. You know with the pressure of working and all. He was in World War II. I don't have a bad relationship with my dad, per se. It's just not much of a relationship. Now my mom, we're really tight.

Dane: She caters to your dad?

Ryan: Yes, for forty-five years. You know, with relationships, maybe I'm trying to find my mom and she don't exist anymore. Women like my mom died out in the early sixties.

Toni: Do you think there is more money for a male escort in being with women or in being with men?

Ryan: Probably men. They have more money, especially here. There are a lot of them and they are really powerful. People don't realize that.

Toni: What do you think about female escorts?

Ryan: I have no problem with it. A lot of times, they're street-level. In fact, they used to have real whores down in Lauderdale. Now they are like crack addicts. Back when I first came down from Boston ten years ago, they would come down for the winter. Just like snowbirds. They were nice girls. They would come from Georgia and the Carolinas. You could spend a few hours with them and they wouldn't take your money. They were hookers with golden hearts. Now it's all messed up.

Toni: If some young guy came up to you and said he wanted to become an escort, what would you tell him? Would you say, go for it?

Ryan: I'd say, be sure you want to do it. I'd say, rent *Midnight Cowboy* and be aware that you are a whore and that there is nothing glamorous about it. But I wouldn't judge him. I'd say, if you are into it, go for it. Go to Miami and Ft. Lauderdale and hang around the hotels. These are places where you find yourself an old broad with money, fuck her, and don't go through an escort service.

Toni: That sounds easy. But if you're not with an escort service, how do you get the point across that the woman is going to have to pay for it? I mean, how do you tell her she'll have to pay?

Ryan: Most of the women I date I end up having them pay for everything. I still do that and I don't know why or how, but I just end up doing it.

Toni: How do you get them to pay for everything?

Ryan: You make it seem like their idea. They do it because they think it's their idea. It's a form of manipulation.

Dane: So if you are planning a date, how does it work?

Ryan: You make them feel real good a couple of times. You figure out what it is that makes them tick and deliver it.

Dane: You mean sexually?

Ryan: Yes. Like I said, it's manipulation. But if you can hit her special spot or whatever, she'll want you. Then you say, "Gee, I don't have any money, but I would be happy to see you." Then they say, "Oh, don't worry about it, I've got money." Then I say, "See you at eight."

With one I said, "Hey, my truck is broke and I need a couple of tires or I'd come over and spend the weekend in Naples with you." So she says, "Go to such and such a station and use my credit card, and get yourself some tires and fill up your tank while you're at it." I said, "OK."

Toni: It's not hard to find women that are willing to do that?

Ryan: I don't think so. Not for me.

Dane: Where in South Florida would a guy go if he was looking for rich, older women?

Ryan: I would go to where all the old people stay, the beaches from Boca to Miami. Check out Ft. Lauderdale. It's all seniors.

When you work through an escort service, it's a little more discreet.

Dane: Is "safe sex" something that you practice?

Ryan: I don't use condoms very often, no.

Toni: Are women more concerned about that these days?

Ryan: They are now. I just don't like condoms. But I'll tell you, I go for a long period of time sometimes without ever having sex. That's a protective measure on my part.

The thing is, I'm at the point where I would like to have a wife and 2.2 kids, the home and the white picket fence. I want to settle down. That is part of my values, you see. After all, I was raised Roman Catholic in a big family, and I want to get back to my roots.

Women's Empowerment and the End of a Revolution

Through the political turbulence of the sixties and into the seventies American women continued to push for change on two fronts: closing the earnings gap and increasing protections on gender-related issues: continued access to abortion and harsher penalties for rape, domestic abuse and sexual harassment. The early seventies saw the passage of an unprecedented number of laws designed to improve the status of women. Women's advocates made headway, bit by bit, using the courts to chip away at gender discrimination.

By the early eighties, women began to look back and examine their place in the Sexual Revolution. "In the 1960s," wrote Gloria Steinem (a one-time Bunny), "any sex outside marriage was called the Sexual Revolution, a nonfeminist phrase that simply meant women's increased availability on men's terms. By the end of the seventies, feminism had brought more understanding that real liberation meant power to make a choice; that sexuality, for women or men, should be neither forbidden nor forced."

The Sexual Revolution fizzled. The last of the company-owned Playboy Clubs closed its doors in 1986. One former Bunny bristles at the title: "Think about it. The word, 'bunny,' is a diminutive of rabbit. A rabbit is a meek, stupid animal that breeds a lot." She reminisced about her experience in the "world's most glamorous waitressing job."

"You walked on parquet-covered concrete slab floors for eight hours in spike heels. The costume was so full of bones and stays, you could shove a sumo wrestler into it and he would have an hourglass figure. When you took it off you had red welts on your ribs that looked like whip marks. It was as uncomfortable as anything great-grandma had to wear. The Bunnies who didn't get enough from nature stuffed Kotex in their bras to make their boobs pillow over the top. While the men were blowing steam out their ears and turning red, the Bunnies counted the minutes till the end of the shift when they could take off those infernal costumes. It was not an erotic or sexual experience. It was the opposite of liberation."

In 1982, the Equal Rights Amendment, introduced in its first form in 1923, fell three short of the thirty-eight states needed for ratification and died. This is what the Amendment said: "Equality of rights under the law shall not be denied or abridged by the United states or any State on account of sex." At the time, two-thirds of the poor in this country were women and the average female college graduate earned the same as the average male whose education ended with high school.

In the mid-eighties, women in business who were passed over for promotions or tracked into lower paying jobs complained about the corporate "glass ceiling." The wage gap then was wider than it had been in 1955. On every front, women were struggling. Access to abortion was under siege from the Religious Right. Domestic violence, according to an F.B.I. report, would affect half of all women at some time in their lives.

But there was progress, too. Rather than beat against the glass, many women started their own businesses, abetted by a booming economy. Between 1982 and 1987, the number of women-owned businesses nearly doubled (from 2.6 million to 4.1 million), a rate of growth that was four times higher than the overall rate of business creation. Profits from these companies netted $278 billion in 1987.

By the end of the decade, women composed more than half of all college students and almost half of all office workers and controlled, though not earned, nearly 80 percent of consumer dollars.

Preston

We interviewed Preston in a rental car on a blustery, snowy Philadelphia day, having met him at the parking lot where he was working his day job as a snow plow driver. He was referred to us by a bartender in a trendy, downtown night spot.

Preston expressed concern about our identity. As a matter of fact, it took five phone conversations to convince him to meet with us. He didn't want to get in trouble with the law because of his nighttime occupation.

He has blond hair, blue eyes and a Midwestern farm boy look. Soft-spoken, he has a slight drawl. He struck us as cautious, for he tends not to reveal too much about himself. A chain smoker, he appeared very nervous at first. But he soon warmed up to us, confessing he "just needed to talk to someone."

He told us that he could never let his friends and family know about his life as an escort, as they would never understand. Preston, like the other men we interviewed, was very much into sex and women in general, always directing answers to Toni even when Dane asked the question.

Toni: Tell us how you got started in the business.

Preston: Through a friend of mine. We were in college and we needed extra money to go out drinking. And just for goofing off. We came up with the idea to put some ads in the *City Paper*, an alternative Philly paper. It took three weeks before we got our first call.

Toni: What was it like the first time someone called you?

Preston: I was nervous. Real nervous.

Dane: What was she like?

Preston: An older lady. About forty-five or fifty.

Toni: What did she look like?

Preston: Tall. Jet black hair. I think her name was Christine. And she wanted to go out for dinner and a few drinks and then she wanted to go to some fancy club.

Dane: Was this in Philly?

Preston: Yeah. We went back to her home and I gave her a leg massage and that was it for the evening. But she spent a total of like nine hundred dollars, somewhere around there.

Dane: In how long a time?

Preston: Six hours.

Toni: What did you do?

Preston: She wanted me to dress up in black pants, black shirt, black tie, shoes, the whole bit, you know.

It was a little nerve-racking, but when you're counting the money, it's like, "I know it's illegal, but you usually don't get in trouble for it. So what the heck," I thought, "do it."

Dane: The cops really don't care?

Preston: Right. I've never heard of an escort getting busted. They'll bust street people, you know, those on the street selling sex. But it seems the higher up the ladder, the less they care.

Toni: Did you have repeat customers that you would see regularly?

Preston: That was maybe six months down the road. You know, you start building up your clientele.

Toni: How often would you see a woman who was a "regular"?

Preston: One I had twice a week. She was divorced. An attorney in Philly.

Dane: An attorney?

Preston: Yeah. Very pretty. Very intelligent.

Toni: Were most of the women married or single?

Preston: There were a few married, some single, some divorced. You get a mix. I think more were divorced, but there were a few married ones, too.

I remember going out to someone's house, and you know, she just wanted to spend some time with me and talk. We were by the fireplace. I think her husband worked a lot or something; he never spent time with her. But that night he unexpectedly came home early, and I was out the door like a bullet!

Dane: Tell us about it.

Preston: Well, we were having sex and I had smoked a joint with her. And, like I said, I don't even usually do drugs, so I was kind of queasy.

And the way her house was set up, it was on a corner, so her house was here and the driveway came into the side. So he was out on the porch or something after he pulled in and I shot out the front door.

Toni: Wow! Close call.

Preston: Nerve-racking, yeah.

Toni: What was your normal rate?

Preston: Around one hundred seventy-five dollars or one hundred and fifty dollars an hour.

Toni: And for most of the dates, was it like a traditional date first? You know, dinner, a movie, or something. Or did you just kind of go to the house and have sex?

Preston: A lot of times I went to the house and then we would go out from there. I would just talk to them, make them feel comfortable. You learn a lot of things from other people.

Dane: For instance?

Preston: You know, who they are, what they've done . . .

Toni: Why do you think the women that were divorced or married, those who were attractive and had some money, why do you think they were paying for this instead of going to a club or hooking up with a neighbor or something?

Preston: To be honest, it's hard to answer that. I'd say their husbands don't pay attention to them. They feel neglected, so they wind up calling someone like me for company or sex.

Dane: How long did you do it for?

Preston: About three years.

Dane: How many different women do you think you've been with in three years? Forty? Fifty?

Preston: It's hard to say. I think close to eighty.

Dane: Eighty?

Preston: Yeah, about eighty in three years.

Toni: How many during the week did you generally see?

Preston: I tried to do ten, fifteen a week. But, like I said, now since I bought equipment for my construction business, you know, I'm trying to get out of it. I've turned down a lot of calls in the last week.

Dane: Why do you want to get out of it?

Preston: I want to stay in the construction business.

Dane: You're getting burnt out being an escort?

Preston: Well, it's just not good to go through life like that. I mean, I wouldn't consider myself a prostitute, but . . . They're all like drug dealers and users and stuff. I wouldn't want to fall into it.

Toni: Did you run into any women who were psychos?

Preston: A couple, yeah. It was nerve-racking. But it was an experience for me, too. One was really into that domination stuff.

Dane: Can you tell us about it?

Preston: It was weird. She wanted to dominate me, speak to me like I was a slave. It was kind of fun in a way, but it was kind of strange, too. Basically, she handcuffed me, put a leash around my neck. Stuff like that.

Dane: Was it at her house?

Preston: Yeah. They lived out in Gladwinne, a very wealthy suburb.

Toni: Did it make you feel uncomfortable?

Preston: Yeah. At the beginning. But then I had a few drinks and settled down.

Dane: What kind of house was it?

Preston: It was a pretty ritzy house, big rooms, nice neighborhood. I was there from like eleven at night until like six or seven in the morning. It was a couple, you know, husband and wife.

Toni: So what happens? The husband watches?

Preston: Yeah. He watched. She dressed up in black stockings with boots and a leather skirt. He was dressed in black G-string underwear. They made me wear a G-string, too. And they put a mask over my face. They had tons of equipment. I mean, these people were really into this kind of thing.

Dane: What kind of stuff were they saying to you?

Preston: They were very strict.

Dane: Calling you names? That kind of thing?

Preston: Yeah. Exactly. Verbal abuse.

Dane: What kind of names did they call you?

Preston: Asshole, bitch, slut. Stuff like that. It was very demeaning. And it was just weird to hear it. All kinds of people act different, but this really rattled me.

Toni: So what were you thinking while this was happening? Like, I wish this were over?

Preston: Yeah, I sure did. I did drink some kind of wine there. I don't know what it was. I'm not a wine drinker.

Dane: Do you think they spiked the wine?

Preston: Yeah, I think so.

Toni: Was the husband participating physically in what was going on? Or was he mostly just watching and saying things?

Preston: She was doing it mostly, being in charge.

Toni: Did she whip you?

Dane: Yeah, she whipped me.

Dane: Hard?

Preston: A couple of times I said, "Hey, you know, you're really carrying this a little too far."

Dane: Was that the weirdest experience you ever went through?

Preston: I had another woman who was also into that. Bondage. Discipline. And she didn't want to let me go. She wanted to keep me for another five or six hours. She had me tied up pretty tight, so it was impossible to get loose.

Toni: How were you tied?

Preston: My hands were tied above my head to the bedpost. If I had to go to the bathroom, she'd tie them right in front of me, tighter. But she was built pretty good. She was strong for a female. No offense here, Toni, but you don't think a female could be that strong. But I guess they could be at times.

Dane: So you were with this woman and your time was up and . . .

Preston: And she says, "No."

Toni: What did you do?

Preston: I was there for like another four hours. I mean, I was playing along with it hoping maybe she'd just let me go. Get tired of it.

Toni: So you tried to talk her out of it?

Preston: I did, right.

Dane: What did you say?

Preston: "Lady, I'll come back tomorrow. I promise," something like that. You just try to make them feel at ease. I'd tell her that I knew she was the boss and stuff. I think she was going through a bad divorce. I found myself feeling sorry for her husband. I mean, this lady was a terror.

Toni: Do you think that she was angry at her husband and taking it out on you?

Preston: Yeah. That thought did cross my mind. The domination was her way of getting back at men for something. I don't know.

Toni: So after a couple of hours of this, when you were getting a little tired of it, what were you saying to her?

Preston: "Enough's enough, lady," I said. Finally after talking to her, it took like maybe three more hours. Finally she said "OK."

Toni: And she let you go?

Preston: Yes.

Toni: Did you ever go back to her?

Preston: She called but I turned her down. I mean, it was fun in a way, but she was really a strong woman.

Toni: Haven't you seen *Fatal Attraction*?

Preston: I know, there's some strange people out there. There really are.

Toni: You mentioned that the first couple had "a lot of equipment." What kind of equipment did they have?

Preston: They had the mask you put over your face. They had things that looked like mitts that go over your hands so you can't move them.

Toni: What were they made of?

Preston: Leather, I think they were leather mitts. So that you can put both your hands in one and you can't do anything.

Toni: It binds your hands or something?

Preston: Right. Exactly.

Toni: Describe the mask? Is it a ski mask type of thing?

Preston: Right. But it's like a hood, a leather hood. It just has the nose and a mouthpiece so you can't see them.

Dane: It must be scary.

Preston: Kind of. But it's also exciting to see a woman dressed up with the nylons and stuff; it turned me on a lot.

Dane: How much did you get paid for that one night?

Preston: I think it was like a twelve hundred dollar deal.

Dane: For how long?

Preston: I was there five or six hours.

Dane: That's pretty good money.

Preston: Yeah. Actually, they were really nice people. Wealthy, too.

Dane: And after this, when it was all over, they reverted back into ordinary, normal people?

Preston: Yeah. They said one time they met someone at a club and they invited him over for drinks, and they held him for a day! And they said the kid didn't know anything about it, like me.

Dane: They held him against his will?

Preston: At first, but then they eased him into it. So they made it work out. I mean, I don't know if that's illegal.

Dane: Yeah. It's called kidnapping.

Toni: Of course. But who's going to talk?

Preston: Yeah. What are you going to say, you know? I mean, I don't care as long as it's not me.

Toni: What was one of your favorite experiences?

Preston: Two girls.

Toni: Did they both pay?

Preston: Yeah. I was there for about five hours.

Dane: Did they contact you in response to your ad?

Preston: Yes. They were actually nice girls. Model material. I was in my glory. When I showed up, I'm like, "Wow!" You know, "Take me!"

Dane: How much did they pay you?

Preston: Eight hundred dollars.

Dane: Did they want to do anything weird or did they just want straight sex?

Preston: Straight sex. They wanted it like twice, three times.

Toni: But everybody was involved at the same time, right? All three of you?

Preston: Right.

Dane: So you had two attractive girls that can probably get anybody they want, and they call up an escort and want to pay for it?

Preston: Yeah. I didn't understand either. It was on a Saturday night. I even asked them, "What are two nice-looking women like you doing calling?" And one says, "Well, we thought it would be fun." The other says, "You know, guys are jerks with us."

Toni: Do you think that's true? Do you think most guys are jerks?

Preston: Well, not all guys. I'm not a jerk to a girl in a bar. You know, I'll talk with her. I'll ask her last name and stuff. It's not like I'm just trying to jump in the sack with her.

Toni: Were most of the dates that you had with women who were a little older?

Preston: There were a lot who were older, like thirty-five up to fifty. Well, for fifty, some people don't look bad, you know.

Toni: Was that ever strange for you, being with a woman that's fifty who could be your mother?

Preston: Yeah, it was. But some of them are really nice people. They're decent.

Toni: If an escort is doing ten or fifteen dates in a week like you were doing, how can you keep up with it? I mean, how can you continue to be excited about all these women, especially some that are older or not as appealing?

Preston: The excitement is in the variety.

Dane: It's not boring, huh?

Preston: Definitely not.

Dane: Did any of the women ever become emotionally attached to you?

Preston: The attorney. She was a repeat. And she was always calling, wanting to see me. I had seen her like, twice in one week. And then a few weeks later I saw her again.

Once I didn't even bother charging her. We just went out for dinner. Of course, she paid for the dinner and everything. It was great. We became really good friends. We still talk, actually.

Dane: But she wanted a relationship with you?

Preston: Yeah, she did. But she's an attorney. A professional. White-collar. And I'm into construction. We come from different worlds.

Dane: You felt out of place in her world?

Preston: Yeah. Some of the people that she's around, they're wealthy, worldly. I just don't fit in. I only look the part. You know what I mean? It's a different social strata, BMWs and mansions, and as an escort, you may be around it, but you're never really in it.

Toni: If most of the women you see are reasonably attractive, and some are pretty young, in their thirties, and they're willing to pay for it, why would you ever want to do traditional dating? Why would you ever want to get out of it?

Preston: You get burnt out. I mean, I really enjoy construction. The money in escorting was great, but you get older and you're like, "Hey, enough's enough." I don't want to go through life like that. I'm getting out.

Dane: How old are you?

Preston: I'm twenty-seven.

Toni: Did you ever have a serious relationship, outside of the customers?

Preston: Yeah. I had a girlfriend.

Dane: Was that before you got into escorting?

Preston: Well, actually I met her while I was doing it.

Toni: Did you tell her what you did?

Preston: Yeah. And she said she'd try to get me out of it.

Dane: But she accepted it for awhile?

Preston: Yeah. She accepted it for two years.

Toni: Was her attitude like, "Wow, you're doing this and getting paid for it; you must be really good sexually"?

Preston: Yeah, she was definitely impressed with it, in the beginning, anyway. And I was impressed with the life too, at first. Most men would love this kind of life. But when you settle down in a relationship, you don't run wild. You have your wild times and then they're over.

Toni: Do you want to get married some day?

Preston: Definitely, yes.

Toni: If you were married, and your wife had been a female escort, do you think that would bother you?

Preston: Yeah. Absolutely, without a doubt it would.

Toni: Why would it bother you if your wife had done it since you had done it?

Preston: I don't know. Maybe because I want her all to myself. Maybe I'm possessive.

Dane: The next woman you get serious about, will you tell her about the business?

Preston: Probably not. If I was going to marry someone, I think then I would tell her.

Toni: What did most women want sexually? Was it traditional sex or really experimental, kinky stuff?

Preston: Both. Some wanted traditional sex, the regular way. A few wanted kinky things, like bondage and discipline. Some had massages, and some just wanted to talk.

Dane: They were lonely?

Preston: Yeah. It was the typical story that you hear — a woman married to a wealthy guy who's not paying any attention.

Toni: Did you have a certain line that you would use with a woman?

Preston: You can't go on using lines, you know. You can't go on bullshitting people. Whatever was brought out, whatever she was talking about, I'd just tell her my true feelings. If you're bullshitting, people catch on eventually.

But you know, I walk away feeling, "I did my best." If that wasn't good enough, well, so be it.

Toni: What do you think is the worst part of the business?

Preston: The hours. You're going out late a lot. And you don't know what's going to happen when you go over to any of these houses. You don't know if it's a setup.

Toni: What do you mean, a setup?

Preston: You could get jumped or killed maybe. There are a lot of freaks out there.

Dane: Did a setup ever happen to you?

Preston: No. If my intuition said back off, I'd back off. What you do is you verify their calls anyway.

Dane: How do you verify the call?

Preston: You check their home phone number through information. See if it's a real number, not a pay phone or something. And if you pull up and it's a shady area, you turn around and walk away. Sometimes you get that gut feeling. Your safety is more important than the money.

Dane: Did you ever get a call from a lady and you met her and then she just turned you off so much you decided to cancel? Or did you take on everybody?

Preston: I've turned a few clients away. I'd just say, "I haven't started here, but I have to run again. Something came up, and I'll call you later."

Dane: Isn't that bullshit?

Preston: No. Well, maybe. But you have to, you know. You have to leave without hurting their feelings.

Dane: Are you still running your ad?

Preston: No. I stopped a couple months ago.

Toni: Tell us about the role-playing you did.

Preston: Role-playing? I did the teacher and the student one. You know, she sits behind a table and everything. She wanted me to write my name like, I don't know, a thousand times or something.

Dane: Did you do that?

Preston: Yeah, I did, to catch up on my penmanship a little bit.

Toni: What did she say?

Preston: She said, "You're staying after school. You have to service me." And the seduction scene came in.

Dane: How old was she?

Preston: She was about thirty-eight. Pretty decent.

Dane: So she called you up in response to your ad, and then asked you on the phone about role-playing?

Preston: Yeah. I talked to her about fifteen minutes on the phone to feel her out. And she told me what she wanted.

Toni: Did you get the feeling she had done this before?

Preston: Oh, yeah. She was good at it. She was a good teacher. She had the spectacles. No panties. And she looked real good in her tutu.

Dane: What age was the oldest woman you were with?

Preston: Fifty-eight. She told me she was fifty-eight. But she looked low forties.

Dane: Were you with any women that were really overweight?

Preston: Yeah. Once. But she had a good personality.

Toni: Does an overweight woman bother you?

Preston: A little bit. But she was a nice person, clean and neat. She wasn't like a rhinoceros or anything.

Toni: Do you think a man can get excited about almost any woman? Because it sounds like you didn't have any trouble.

Preston: I think that all guys have certain types of women they like. Me, I like most women. They'd have to be pretty ugly to turn me off.

Toni: What do you think is the best thing about being an escort?

Preston: Definitely the money.

Dane: What do you think you can make in a week in your busiest times?

Preston: You could do a good three or four thousand a week if you push it.

Dane: Consistently? Every week?

Preston: And besides having an ad, you could go to clubs and expand your clientele.

Toni: If a guy wanted to become an escort, what kind of advice would you give him?

Preston: Just watch out. Be careful. And don't make a life out of it. Actually it would depend on the person. But I could give them some pointers.

Toni: Sounds like you had a lot of fun in it and earned some good money. Do you feel it's had some negative effects too?

Preston: Yeah. I feel guilty sometimes. I feel like I'm not really contributing something in life. But then other times I figure, "Hey, these women need someone like me. It's business." I don't know; it's confusing.

Toni: You said some women were into domination. Did any of them want you to hurt them?

Preston: Yeah. One. I turned her down. I couldn't.

Toni: What did she want you to do?

Preston: Tie her up and slap her around. I couldn't do it. I said, "Sorry, call someone else."

Dane: Did she offer you more money?

Preston: Yeah. She offered me double and then triple. I said, "Look, I can't hit a girl." No way. You have your limits.

Dane: The ad you ran in the *City Paper*. What did you say in it? Do you remember exactly?

Preston: I said: "6 feet 1 inch, blond hair, blue eyes, 160 pounds, clean and discreet, seeks generous female for close encounters. Call——" We changed it every few weeks, and we always got a response. I was getting fifteen calls a week for awhile. As soon as the phone started ringing and my beeper started going off, it was like a cash register. But now, I'm too busy with starting my business.

Dane: So you don't really care anymore?

Preston: No.

Dane: Would you say that there's a good market for this, if a guy wanted to get into it?

Preston: Yes. There are a lot of women out there who aren't afraid of paying men for sex. If a guy wants to get into it, and he has the tools, mentally and physically, he can make as much money as he wants. And here in Milwaukee, man, there's a lot of ladies willing to pay.

Dane: Do you think if you fell on hard times, Preston, you'd get back into it?

Preston: It would really depend. Bottom line, yeah, I would, if I was in need. But one of the things I think about is diseases. I'm always careful, but you never know. Thank God, I'm fine.

Adrian

We met Adrian in a coffee shop in Greenwich Village. He responded to the ad we placed in the Village Voice *seeking escorts to interview. He was very cautious and a bit wary of our intentions. While we taped this interview, he taped it on his own recorder. "Just to make sure everything's on the up and up," he said.*

His Cherokee and Italian heritage give Adrian his unusual looks. You could easily guess he works as a model. At 6 feet, 170 pounds, he is lean and sleek. His shoulder length black hair is thick and shiny, and his chestnut eyes sparkle. Actually, he seems much older than his twenty-four years, for he's been around and is very street-wise.

Adrian: I don't want my name to be printed.

Toni: Your name won't be used. You're gonna be someone else.

Dane: What name would you like?

Adrian: Adrian.

Toni: What name do you go by in your ad in the paper?

Adrian: The name I use is "Eros."

Dane: How long have you been in this business?

Adrian: On and off, two years. Actually, I have a "real" job too, modeling. And its funny, if you talk to just about anybody who's a professional model, they'll say that modeling is just a legal form of prostitution! So anyway, I model when I'm not doing this.

I'll tell you one thing, though. I've been with two escort agencies and I'll never work with another again.

Toni: How come?

Adrian: One of the heads of the agency was more intent on getting me into bed than anything else. Which is fine, if that's her business, you know. I guess she wanted to test the merchandise or something! You know, its one thing to strip down and show your body. I have no problem with that, but you know, there's been times where I had absolutely the worst clients in the world and I just got so depressed. I called my mom and I'm like, "Mom, I had this really bad client today." And she's like, "What happened?" And, you know, I tell people that my mom knows and they just think that's the weirdest thing in the world.

Toni: Your mom does know?

Adrian: She knows everything.

Dane: How does she feel about it?

Adrian: She's fine. The thing that she's really worried about is my safety.

Toni: Tell us about some of your clients.

Adrian: Well, I do both women and men. And there are very big differences between the women and men clients, huge differences. Namely, the men are more concerned about penis size. They'll say, "Well, how big are you?" Women are much more in touch with a sensitive side. The men are notoriously cheap, too. I mean, I got guys calling me just intent on talking my price down. And I'm like, "You know, this is not K–mart blue light special, you pay the fee."

Dane: What was your first client like?

Adrian: She saw an ad I put in the paper. And afterwards, she started recommending me. Which surprised me, you know, that someone would actually admit to someone else, "Yes, I had an escort, liked him, recommend him." Kind of like you'd recommend your plumber, you know. It was like, I got a call and she says, "Well, my friend, Catherine, told me about you." I start laughing and she goes, "What's so funny?" And I say, "Well, its kind of strange to me that someone's gonna say, 'Yeah, you should try this one out.'

So anyway, this woman has a mansion in Scarsdale, and I'm like, in total awe. She's British, maybe fifty-four, very nice, polite. But she was very much into playing games. Role playing, I guess you'd call it. And the very first time I saw her, she had no clothes on, but she had chains and leather and nipple clamps, the whole nine yards! She had a dog collar on, she had a leash. I didn't even have to get undressed.

Toni: Can you describe her? What did she look like?

Adrian: Very petite, blondish, blue eyes, young-looking. Kind of porcelain, you know, very, very pasty white skin.

Dane: Ghostly.

Adrian: But very nice. She did not look her age. Put it that way. Fifty-four is not old, but I know some that are like prunes. So she was very skinny, busty. When I saw that, my first thought was: boob job, because I have enough friends who are strippers and dancers to know a boob job when I see one. But I'm not gonna say, "Oh, that's a boob job? You had a good surgeon, or something."

Anyway, what happened was I was in the living room, she was in the kitchen. All of a sudden I heard these chains. It sounded like a ghost haunting the house. And I walked in there, and she had shackles on her feet, chains in between her feet. A belt on her waist, a chain came up to the belt. She had nipple clamps with a chain going from nipple to nipple.

I remained dressed through the entire thing. There was, you know, "slave," "master," "bitch," "do it". And actually she was licking my boots clean, these boots in fact.

I'm standing above her, wearing a pair of jeans, and she's on her back and my feet are right outside of her head. She's just going from side to side, licking my boots. My first thought was, I hope I didn't step in any dogshit! You know, it would not have been cool.

Toni: This is at her house?

Adrian: Yes. Fireplace is going and it's a romantic atmosphere. It was kind of strange because it's like there was mood music going. A classical piece I wasn't familiar with. And no lights other than the fire, and I'm doing this to her, and I was wondering if this is a form of romance for her, which I thought was really interesting. And I talked with her afterwards about it, and she's just experimenting. She says at her age, she wants to make sure that the spice is not disappearing anywhere. And the main reason why she wanted to see me was because I had long hair and I was, as she had heard, "prettier than a lot of the other guys." And also because I wasn't six-feet-five and I wouldn't tower over her so much to where she would feel threatened.

Anyway, nothing was exchanged: no bodily fluids, no oral, no sex, or anything. And I think that was maybe her test, to see how I would react to her outfit before she would trust me to do anything else. That's cool. The less sexual activity I have to do, the better.

Dane: Why?

Adrian: It's very draining.

Dane: Did you see her again?

Adrian: Yes. The second time I saw her, I still didn't dress up. I was in a pair of slacks and a sweater. I went there and I actually had dinner with her. We were talking a little business. I try not to pry too much, but we were on a level to where it was, like, no problem. I mean, she knew my real name by that time.

Toni: The trust was growing.

Adrian: Yeah. And I felt close to her because she reminded me of my mother.

Dane: Your mother?

Adrian: Yeah. My mother's not that old, but she just kind of reminded me of her. Anyway, there was a part of me that was having a problem with it, with going over there knowing that something might happen because I was like, "My mom!" So we had dinner. It started to go a little bit hotter and heavier, the fireplace was going, and she proceeded to go down to her knees. She's looking up at me with these lusty eyes and then, pop! Out come her teeth!

Dane: Oh, my God! How embarrassing!

Adrian: Shock. Because my mom has an upper plate too, and that's what clinched it for me. I'm like, "My God, my mother's gonna give me a blow job." (laughs) Honest to God's truth, that was the best blow job in the world.

Toni: Did you almost want to laugh when the dentures flew out of her mouth?

Adrian: I did, you know, but I kind of looked down instead. So, by that time I was just like, "OK, I've seen everything, I've heard everything"... until she pulled out the strap-on.

Dane: The what?

Adrian: The strap-on dildo. She wanted to do me, which I had never had that done before. And I was a bit thrown by that one. I said, "Uh, are you sure?" She said, "Oh, yeah." She's, like, she bought it, she's saved it, it's still in the packaging. And I thought, I guess this must mean that I'm pretty open-minded and daring. So we went through with it.

Toni: You did?

Adrian: Yeah, it was interesting.

Dane: Would you do it again?

Adrian: With her, yeah.

Toni: Was she pretty aggressive or fairly gentle?

Adrian: She wanted to be demeaned, humiliated. Not to the point of getting into water sports, but... and she wanted to humiliate me, too.

Dane: Did you find it demeaning when she was doing this to you? Was she saying things to belittle you?

Adrian: Well, she was saying, "You like it, don't you?" And I'm like, "Yeah."

Dane: But what were you feeling emotionally?

Adrian: Nothing. It didn't even seem real.

Toni: But you would do it again?

Adrian: Yeah. Well, you know, she had pretty good moves for a woman.

Toni: For a woman?

Adrian: Yeah.

Dane: So you think a man can satisfy another man better than a woman can satisfy a man?

Adrian: It's true.

Dane: You really believe that?

Adrian: Yeah.

Toni: Why?

Adrian: Look, it's the same as a woman with a woman. It's better because women know another woman's pressure points. They know where everything is. A guy knows what path to follow, what vein to put pressure on. He knows that if you are on the head a certain way, you can either make him ejaculate faster or you can hold him back. You know where to touch.

Dane: The same sex knows their bodies better?

Adrian: Exactly. My mom has been with women before and she told me, "It's great, you know." And I said, "Are you seeing anybody now?" And she goes, "Yeah. This woman who drives a Harley named Maureen."

Toni: Your mom? She's really open, huh?

Adrian: Incredibly open. Yeah, and so she told me the same thing that I said. Women know how to do it, but there's something that's missing, obviously, that you can't get with the same sex.

Dane: Tell us about your mother. She sounds fascinating.

Adrian: She is. She's a character. She's forty-four, exactly twenty years older than me. I just turned twenty-four. She was adopted, and she was the black sheep of the family. I mean, she threw her brothers through glass windows and stuff. She was a hellion.

Dane: She's Indian?

Adrian: Cherokee. My dad was from Italy. She's got a very nasty temper which she's learned to control, which I ended up picking up from her. Because I've got a terrible temper.

Dane: Does your mother know you are bisexual?

Adrian: Sure.

Dane: She's bisexual, too?

Adrian: Yeah. And you know, I thought three years about this business before getting into this. I wanted to make money, and even if I did what I went to school for, marketing, I would not even remotely make as much money as what I do now. Because of my age, they would start me off in the lowest position possible, regardless of how good I am. So I thought about it for three years, and I told my mom, and she's like, "OK. Be careful." She calls me more often now because she's a little bit more concerned. And whenever I have a bad experience, I call her up. There was one time I had such a bad time with it I was in tears all night.

Toni: What happened?

Adrian: It's, see, it's physically and emotionally draining. Its so easy to see why so many escorts get involved in cocaine and other drugs. Because really, these people who call... When I worked with the agency, sure I felt a little safer, but at the same time, I was at their mercy. The only way to do this is really to go out on your own. Besides, I had the feeling that some of these agency owners were drug running, and I was like, you know, if I got caught into something like that, sure he'd bail me out. It would be hush-hush money, but its like, who's to say that if I'm in a limousine or something like that, I'm not gonna get a drive-by shooting and end up dead. But as far as emotionally exhausting, well, I did six appointments in one day.

That literally devastated me. I mean, I'm twenty -four, I can go. I have no problem to keep going. But there's so much of it that is false.

Dane: What do you mean?

Adrian: Well, if I'm sitting across from somebody, I have to pretend to be so interested in what they're saying. I've had lawyers, deans of universities, bank presidents. And emotionally what it does is, it eats you up. You're sitting there, listening to this person. And you're bored to death and you couldn't care less and you pretend. And outwardly you're going, "Oh, that's so interesting." And inwardly you're going, "Blah blah blah." A lot of times you get people flaunting their money, their power. They're not talking with you, they're talking at you, and you have to sit there and be interested because that's your job. And above all else, they want you to worship them.

One time I was at dinner with this client. He was telling me his life story, how some awful woman had done him wrong, what the problem was, how it affected him, how much she took from him. And my first reaction was like, "The money is not this important. You got what you deserved. You're an asshole." And I left. That was it.

Toni: How much do you charge for six appointments in one day?

Adrian: Six in a day, I charge around two hundred dollars for each appointment.

Dane: Twelve hundred bucks a day.

Adrian: Twelve hundred bucks a day. Mind you, cold weather brings out the weirdos because there's snow, and they don't want to go out, so the main thing that they do is call you up and they hang up on you. And there's been death threats...

Toni: To you?

Adrian: Oh, yeah. I'm not the only one that's gotten them.

Dane: Why do you think they're doing that?

Adrian: Because they're just being assholes. Because they know that you're an easy target as an escort. You know, it's not hard for someone to find out where you live. All they have to do is get hold of phone records.

Dane: Do you think there are people that hate escorts?

Adrian: Sure. It's the exact same thing as when a guy harasses someone because he's gay. It's because he's probably gay himself.

So I'm an easy target. Granted I cater to women, but I also do a few men.

Toni: What do you like about women?

Adrian: The mental connection. Its kind of nice to be able to talk to someone on an intellectual level and say, "You know, this is what I think about global warming," and then go have fun. But with guys it's like, "Come in, drop your pants." That's it.

Toni: Not a lot of conversation.

Adrian: Right. And even if you do, it's duh... And also, the fact that men are extremely cheap.

Dane: Well, maybe the best kind of person, then, would be androgynous, do you think?

Adrian: That's why I have it so easy. It's interesting, too, that most guys that call want a very smooth body. So, being a model, I already have to shave practically everything anyway.

Personally, though, I will not date a younger girl.

Dane: Why?

Adrian: Because I think that if a girl has to pay for it, not that there's something wrong with her, but I think there's some sort of distrust there. I mean, I don't trust anybody. I treat all of my clients like this. A girl, really regardless of what she looks like, can go out and get laid anytime she wants.

Toni: But what about the distrust part of it? What do you mean by that?

Adrian: If a girl has to pay for it, I wouldn't trust her because it would be so easy for her to say, "Rape!" And I would not be able to defend myself on that because they would take her word for it.

With men, you don't have to worry about that. Men come in, boom, off go the pants. The girls, though, I wouldn't trust. Tell you the truth, I don't date women younger than twenty-eight.

Toni: And you're twenty-four?

Adrian: Yes. And, basically, it's because of the fact that when you hit a certain age, I think it's around late twenties, early thirties, you really start to get your priorities straight. I'm not a club-goer. I don't do drugs. I don't smoke. I don't drink. I get up at five o'clock in the morning to work out. So, it's very important for me to have somebody that knows where their priorities are, to have a stable job. They pay for their own bills. I have a job. I pay for my own. That's important to me.

And I have gone out with women who are younger. It's just something that doesn't interest me. I find older people more interesting. I'm not saying like seventy-nine, which I did have one of those once, but it was a man.

Toni: Tell us about that experience.

Adrian: I got set up by an old boyfriend of mine. Because he called on my answering machine one time, "Hi, this is Ron, blah, blah, saw your ad, call me back, blah blah." I'm like, "Oh, my God." So I called him up and I said, "Hi, this is Adrian." I recognized his voice right away, even though I hadn't talked to him in like two years. He goes, "Hi, kid, how ya doing?" And I said, "Well, I'm just returning your call." And he goes, "Uhh...?" It was like twenty seconds of silence. I was waiting for it to dawn on him. And finally he goes, "Oh my God!" You know, because he dialed me as an escort. He goes, "That was your ad?!" I said, "Yeah." And I laughed. Be careful out there, you never know who you might be calling!

Anyway, we got into this discussion and he wanted me, too, and he's like, "Do you remember my neighbor Tom?" I'm like, "Yeah, the old man that lived two doors down." And he's like, "Well, he would really like to have a young boy strip for him." And I'm like, "OK, no problem."

I got there. When I was done, I went back over to Ron's house, bullshit! I was about ready to kill him because he didn't tell me that the old man had one of his legs amputated. That old man was chasing me around in a wheelchair.

Toni: He was chasing you in a wheelchair??

Adrian: Well, I wasn't running, but I'm like, "I'm supposed to strip for you and that's it." And he was like, he didn't have a tooth in his mouth either. I mean he's an old man. Like he's going, "Mem, mem, mem," like that.

And he wanted me to kiss him, and I'm like, "Tom, I don't kiss."

I get weirdos, I'm not kidding. So, when I got back to Ron's apartment, I'm like, "I'm gonna kill you." And he was up in the shower, and he started laughing and he goes, "Oh. Oh."

So, old Tom wants to see me again.

Toni: Would you see him again?

Adrian: Oh, I don't know, maybe when I get really desperate for the money.

Toni: How much did he pay you for that?

Adrian: One-fifty.

Dane: Just for the stripping?

Adrian: Yeah. And, it was kind of funny. It was a charge, I must admit. It was something to really write down in my journal. I'm like, my God! Because this guy, he's just got a stump and a leg, in a wheelchair and gumming all the while!

As far as young girls go, I just won't. The guys, I've had all the way down to seventeen call me up, and I won't even do that just because they're underage.

Dane: Adrian, has your mother ever done escorting?

Adrian: No. She's done go-go dancing though, so, technically, I guess you could say it's almost the same thing.

Toni: Does she live here?

Adrian: She's in Michigan. I don't think she ever had a desire to do escort. She could sure make more money, though. In my very first weekend, I made about fifteen hundred bucks, and I make more in a weekend than what she does in a month.

Dane: So she doesn't disapprove of what you do?

Adrian: No. She knows me to be very, very open and extremely cautious. Even if she did disapprove, I've always been really good at cutting off sources. I mean, it would be hard to cut your mother off, but I mean, there were times that we had some big blowups. She knows my temper. I threw knives at her one time because she pissed me off, so …

Dane: Knives?

Adrian: Yeah, I just happened to be in the next room and she just said something I didn't like, and I was having a bad day.

Dane: What did she say?

Adrian: I don't even remember. I was still in high school and I threw a couple of knives, and she's like, "You little fucker. I don't believe you did that." So, I've learned to control that aspect.

But I don't think she's extremely happy with what I do. Every now and then she goes, "When you gonna go get a real job?" And I'm like, "Well, Mom, technically this is a job, you know. I'm getting paid for doing professionals."

I tell her about some of the clients I had. Like there was this guy I had done, twenty-nine, complete virgin with guys, in AA, and I told her that if you look at it in a certain way, it's really a service to these people who don't have self-esteem.

Basically, I'm taking these used pieces of toilet paper, that people forgot to throw into the toilet, and my job is to sort of mold origami out of it. Regardless of how messy it is. That's difficult because sometimes your hands slip and slide all over the place. And there's been a few times where I'm like, "You're beyond help," and just take the scissors to it. You flush.

So that's the way I described it, and she's like, "Well, I think it's good that you can make these people feel better."

I said, "It's good you think that way, because making these people feel better a lot of times makes me feel really bad."

Toni: Drains you.

Adrian: It's emotionally draining.

Dane: Do you feel like you're something of a psychologist when you're with them?

Adrian: Very much.

Toni: How do you screen your calls?

Adrian: There's been times with a potential client where I was on the phone with her for ninety minutes because I want to know who I'm getting involved with. My clientele rate is 90 percent return. I have very high return because of the fact that I talk to them. Screen them as best I can.

Dane: Did the women you were with ever become emotionally involved with you?

Adrian: No, it's been the guys. The women are very businesslike, and I consider the women to be a lot smarter then men, more emotionally stable and more in tune with my feelings. Because there were times when I had no energy to do it, and, obviously, I'm like, "Sorry." They'd say, "If it can't be done, it can't be done, we'll just talk." With a guy you wouldn't get that.

But the women, I don't find them more emotionally attached, mainly because the women I've dealt with have been smarter. The one from England has a Fortune 500 company. So, she's a brain, doesn't let things like that get in the way.

Dane: But a woman like that, successful, independent, probably attractive. Why is she paying to have sex?

Adrian: There's probably not too many other guys that she would be able to date if she whipped out the strap-on dildo and tried to shove it up his rear end.

I asked her that night why she doesn't date. And she told me she's got a business; she doesn't have the time. She's fifty-four. Even if she had the time, she wouldn't go clubbing. It's not her style. She's ambitious, aggressive, and I find her interesting.

Toni: What kinds of things did you learn from her?

Adrian: When you get into this job, you become very jaded. I don't trust anybody now. I'm very particular who I hang out with and I don't waste my time. She showed me you can still be successful in what you're doing and it's nothing demeaning to have to pay for something like this. Because the fact is she can't find what she's looking for. She has money, and granted money can't buy love. But she's not looking for love. She wasn't trying to buy affection from me, she was just trying to buy me for the weekend. I have no problem with that. So I learned a lot from her. And I liked her.

Dane: What if it's someone you don't like?

Adrian: If it's someone I'm not remotely interested in, they're paying for a service, so I'll try to appear interested. I literally had to get rid of all the clocks in my living room because I find myself staring at them. And that's bad. It's not good business and it's certainly not good for me emotionally, because I'm, like, after I'm done with a client, I have to clean the house again. I'm like, "Oh, got to get rid of the karma."

Dane: What is your workout routine? Obviously you have to stay in shape for both the modeling and escorting.

Adrian: Life weights, cardiovascular. I have to do everything at home because I don't have time to go to a gym.

Toni: How many hours a day?

Adrian: One or two. Six days a week.

Dane: What do you think is the best part of being an escort? And what is the worst?

Adrian: The best part is the money. There's no denying it, and anybody who says that money is not the best part is a liar. The second best is that I've made a lot of great friends. My social circle is around the modeling industry. Models are really, really fake. Cocaine, drugs, smoking. They're flubbers. So I've met some good people.

The worst thing is the emotional toll that it takes on you. A therapist once told me that working escort was "easy money." I couldn't believe it when I heard that. I'm like, "Jennifer," and she goes, "Yeah?" And I said, "Well, not to really demean you, but I would like you to know something. This is not easy money. Granted I can make three hundred dollars an hour, but you better believe that there's something that is disappearing from me each time I've spent time with someone that I don't care for. And sex is important to me. I don't like to just have to go out and give it to anybody."

You have to understand that what I'm doing is really customer service. And I know if this person likes me, is attracted to me, and wants to see me more often, I'll make more money. So what I do is maintain my customer service to the utmost level. I have some friends that have hired escorts before and they're like, "My God, I just had the worst experience. This guy came in and he said, 'Next time more money and more cocaine and we'll have more fun.'"

Obviously, that guy's not going to get called back again. And that's probably why it's so emotionally draining for me because I have to basically shove Adrian all the way back and front this person who, being very chameleonlike, can handle it. But after so long it's kind of hard to make this person disappear and let me come back out again. I mean, when I go home, I can just relax, wash my hair, lay around like a pig.

Dane: You're not on stage anymore.

Adrian: Right, exactly. That's the thing, I'm on stage all the time. Being an escort and being a model. My appearance is always important.

Dane: Some escorts, they feel a lot of guilt being in this line of work. Do you ever feel that?

Adrian: Maybe it could be guilt and I just can't recognize it because I'm Catholic. And we're used to it. But, frankly, I consider guilt to be a very destructive emotion. And what's the point of destroying yourself? Only you can build yourself up. Other people will try to destroy you. And you let them or you don't. So maybe it is a form of guilt that's chafing away at me.

Toni: You also believe you're doing these people some good, too, and maybe you are.

Dane: It's like being a bartender. Certain professions require you to be a good listener.

Adrian: True. I view it as that more than anything else.

Dane: Have you ever been with a couple?

Adrian: Yes. Actually, that's my appointment today .

Toni: Do you like that, when it's more than one? Is it more money?

Adrian: Of course. I charge this client a rate and a half, four hundred and fifty dollars for an hour.

Dane: Is this the first time you've done it?

Adrian: No. A friend of mine is an escort too, and we were both hired by this guy once. He wanted a male and a female escort at the same time so we did it. And it's kind of interesting because she and I knew each other and we had this guy in the bed; she was in front and I was in back. She's pretty much sitting down on his face and I'm behind him and he can't see anything, so we're like making faces at each other and we kind of started to laugh! But as soon as one of us started to laugh, it was like he would stop. And then we're going, "Oh, yes, good," and stuff. It was kind of funny because she's supposed to be writhing in ecstasy and I'm supposed to be having a very ecstatic experience, and we're like nodding off. I had to take my watch off and everything, and it was funny.

Dane: Has being an escort taken a toll in terms of sex not being as exciting for you?

Adrian: Oh yes. It's not really as interesting anymore. If I go three days without it, I'm like, "Thank you, Lord." My friends don't get it. They're like, "We've always thought about escorting." And I'm like, "Why?" Oh, they say, "Because it must be so exciting you get to have sex all the time." And I'm like, "But that's all it is, just sex." Sex is really nothing. I could have a lot more fun by myself eight times a day. Granted, I wouldn't get paid, but…

Dane: So you look at it as a job. It pays well.

Adrian: I've even found myself walking through the house telling the dog, "God, I hate my job." And that's how I view it. I hate my job. When my business phone rings, I'm like, "Damn! "

Toni: And then you pick up the phone and put on the act, huh?

Adrian: Yeah. It's like, "Can you describe yourself? How big are you?" And I'm like, "Come on! " Because when most of the guys see you, size means nothing. And that's true of women, too. Size means nothing.

Toni: What's the most important part to women?

Adrian: Companionship. A lot of women call, and say, "Well, I'm just looking for someone to talk to." Three days ago, a woman picked me up in a stretch white limo, on my street. Now, I live in an excellent neighborhood, but we don't have stretch limos coming by. I'm like, "You might want to get rid of this car for awhile. Everybody's going to know what you're doing. I mean, it's parked right in front of my house."

Toni: Are you ever offered trips or gifts?

Adrian: Yeah, I get gifts. One of my clients, I saw her last Sunday, offered to buy me a car.

Toni: No kidding?

Adrian: She's got three cars: a Porsche, a Shelby Mustang, a Mercedes. Her father was on the stock exchange or something. She's like, "When you want to go to New York, let me know. I'll get you an apartment." I have a real problem accepting stuff like that.

Toni: Are you going to take her up on it?

Adrian: I don't know. Granted, I'm spoiled, but still …that's a pretty big gift.

Dane: You have trouble accepting gifts. Do you have trouble accepting compliments as well?

Adrian: Interesting question. I don't take compliments well at all. I say, "Thanks," but being in the modeling industry you hear them all the time. "Oh, you're beautiful, you're gorgeous, this outfit looks great on you, you're so hot." So much of it is bull. And I hear that too when I meet a client. "You're beautiful." I'm like, "Thanks." Yawn. Well, of course, I don't say it like that. I go, "Thank you." But inside, I'm like, "Blah blah blah."

Toni: Do people like the fact that you're a model?

Adrian: Yeah. I was thinking about taking the word "model" out of my ad because of the fact that they call up and they're like, "So, are you a real model?" I'm like, "I'm signed with an agency." Blah blah blah.

Dane: What does your ad say?

Adrian: "Exotic Italian bad boy model available for erotic encounters." I don't give out measurements. I don't say, "Well-hung white available" or something because I don't want those kind of people calling. Of course, you still get them.

Sometimes the people go, "What is an erotic encounter?" And I'm like, "It's all in your mind. You know, it could be a full body massage with me just lightly gliding my hair across your body. I have shoulder-length, dark brown hair." By the way, women are very much into that.

Dane: They like long hair?

Adrian: Definitely. The guys not so much.

Toni: Really?

Adrian: Yes. I get more clients from women than men. But I've found guys do not like long hair. When they aren't interested on the phone it's because of the fact that I've told them I've got long hair. That's a fact. I say it's chin-length; they just hang up. And you get so many of those, the hang ups, and that is so demeaning. I'm gonna get Caller ID soon and when I do, I'm gonna call these people back and go, "How does it feel?" and hang up on them. It's really annoying.

Toni: How much longer do you think you'll work as an escort?

Adrian: Not for long. As soon as I get signed by a modeling agency in New York, I'm gone. But if I end up not getting jobs in New York, I may have to get back into it.

Dane: Can you give us an idea of what your income is per year?

Adrian: Well, for the last six months, I've made three grand a week. I guess that's seventy-five thousand dollars. In a year, I guess I'll make one hundred and fifty thousand dollars.

Dane: What do you do for your taxes?

Adrian: I put "model." Well, technically, that's what I am. At least, part of the time.

Toni: What kind of modeling jobs have you done?

Adrian: Retail, runway stuff, you know. The last show I did was two months ago. I haven't had the time to concentrate on it because I've been so busy doing this. But, you know, I make much more money doing this than modeling. Something really fucked up about that. I did one runway show where I was modeling a chain metal top with a metal skirt. I wasn't wearing anything underneath.

Dane: A metal skirt?

Adrian: Yeah, it's the latest thing. And I was really flopping around the runway that night. Got a few phone numbers as well.

Toni: Is there a need for more guys out there to be escorts?

Adrian: There is definitely a market for male escorts. Like in New York, my friends make between three hundred and five hundred bucks an hour. That's not bad. But from what I hear about California, you make less because there's so many escorts.

Toni: So there are a lot of women out there looking for male escorts?

Adrian: All over the place! In the suburbs, the more affluent areas.

Toni: And you don't take on young women clients even when they call you up?

Adrian: Younger women, no. Older women, always.

Dane: How many appointments do you have a week?

Adrian: It varies. I get maybe fifteen, twenty calls every day. Not all those are vocal contacts, some just hang up. But on vocal contacts, I would probably take three-fourths of those who call. A lot of times I can't accept the job because I'm already booked.

This one woman called me four times. Four times in one week. I told her to meet me at a certain restaurant, at a certain time, and then I couldn't make it. And she still called me back! That was really cool, considering I didn't show up.

Dane: If a friend of yours said, "Adrian, I want to get into the business," what would you tell him?

Adrian: Go for it. Make some money and then get out.

Toni: What do you think is the most important attribute for a male escort to have to be successful?

Adrian: Nerves of steel and thick skin. I've got both, but it really grates after a while. You can only have so many people chopping away at your shield until there's going to be some sort of dent in it.

Dane: How do you feel they're chopping away at you?

Adrian: That's a tough one. It's a combination of calls and hang ups, or people that call just to get you on the phone for phone sex. There's tons of that.

Toni: For free.

Adrian: Yeah. I'm like, "Send me over a check if you want to talk." There's been times I did it just because I was so annoyed. Like last weekend. Got this woman on the phone. She's getting all hot and bothered.

I'm like, "You know what you should do now?" She's like, "Oooh, tell me." "Take a cold shower," and I hung up on her.

I don't want to become like a lot of other escorts that do that kind of stuff. But once in awhile, you sure realize why they do it.

Toni: Can just about any guy become an escort?

Adrian: It's not for everybody. I have a friend who's done it for a month and he's already burnt out. He's twenty-five and can't do it anymore. It's just too demanding, and I think part of it is that he wants to look for someone to settle down with, and you can't do it when you work escort. This takes a toll on relationships. I don't know if I'll ever have one. Maybe I've been in the business too long, but it sure isn't anything I want anymore. Nope, I'm just gonna rake in some more money, coast on my looks for awhile, cash in on the modeling, and get to L.A.

Mom

Adrian referred to his mother so often during his interview that we asked if he could arrange for us to speak with her. She agreed to a phone interview. Soft-spoken and with a southern drawl, she gave us an interesting and unique perspective — that of a mother with a son in the business.

Dane: What would you like your name to be in the book?

Mom: Call me what "Adrian" calls me, Mom.

Toni: OK, Mom. How do you feel about your son Adrian being an escort?

Mom: Well, it's his life. He's over twenty one. I'm not saying that I really like the idea because he's got a lot of intelligence. He can do something else. But as long as he wants to, it's up to him.

Dane: What kind of concerns do you have?

Mom: Safety concerns, I guess, because he's never really been a big person. And there's a lot of weirdos out there. So I do worry at times.

Toni: Do you ever have any moral issues with what he's doing?

Mom: I did at first. I don't think it's right to be doing this, but I can't say too much because none of us is perfect.

Toni: How did you feel when he first told you what he's doing for a living?

Mom: I about fell off the couch!

Toni: How do you feel now?

Mom: He's doing real well for himself. He's taking care of his business and his life, and that costs a lot of money. He's living pretty good.

Dane: Would it bother you if your friends knew what Adrian does?

Mom: No, because about everyone I know is pretty open-minded. And if they didn't like it, they're entitled to that opinion.

Dane: Can you tell us about Adrian's background?

Mom: He was raised without a father. So he had a hard life, in that way. But he didn't go without very much either.

Dane: I think he told us he was spoiled.

Mom: Spoiled rotten.

Dane: He also told us he inherited a bad temper.

Mom: Oh! Yes, I guess he did. Well, it's kind of calmed down now, now that I'm getting older.

Toni: Would you say that he had a pretty liberal upbringing?

Mom: Yeah. Because when I was young, I used to party a lot. And there wasn't too much that surprised me. So I tried to raise him where he wouldn't have any prejudices. He's very tolerant, I think.

Toni: How do you feel his childhood was different from yours?

Mom: Well, I went through a hell of a lot more. At times it was very tough but I won't bore you. Anyway, he didn't have it too bad.

Dane: Where would you like to see Adrian in five years?

Mom: A model. Or an artist. Or a musician. I'd like to see him using any of his talents. He's very talented.

Toni: He's very attractive, too. Half Cherokee and half Italian, that's some combination! He got the Cherokee from you?

Mom: Yeah. We're both very unique in our looks.

Toni: Now that you know what the life of an escort is like, because Adrian's been in it, do you think that if you were Adrian's age and you needed some money, you would consider working as an escort?

Mom: To be completely honest, I probably would. I mean, back when I was young, I didn't think of stuff like that. You worked, most of it slave labor. And I think I would, if I had it to do all over again. Sorry, baby, but they make a lot of money.

Dane: Do you think the business has helped Adrian at all?

Mom: Yeah, I think so.

Dane: How would you say it has helped him?

Mom: Well, it sure as hell helped him financially. And he's beginning to check into other people's morals and just basically learning a hell of a lot.

Toni: He also expressed to us that he is getting experience in becoming a good listener because so many clients tell him their problems.

Mom: Oh, yeah. I talk to him about that. He says sometimes it's such a mental strain, always listening to people's problems. Every now and then he's got to get away from that because always hearing other people's problems will just drive you crazy.

Toni: Mom, this is your chance to tell the public what you think. Clear up any misconceptions about the business. As a mother with a son in the business, what do you want people to know?

Mom: Well, just because he's doing what he's doing, it doesn't make him a bad person. He just wants to make a living like anyone else, and it's not that easy to be able to do what you really like. He wants to get into the arts. He's so gifted. I look at the escorting as only a temporary thing.

But the truth of life is you always have to pay somebody, one way or the other. You always do.

He doesn't think he's doing anything wrong. He's just taking care of his life. I know he doesn't want to stay in this line of business forever. But I also don't think anybody ought to be judging anybody, because different strokes for different folks. We all do what we gotta do to get by.

Dane: How often do you two talk?

Mom: Oh, at least once or twice a week.

Toni: He tells you about most of the appointments he goes on?

Mom: Well, let's just say he tells me a few things. I don't think he wants to reveal too much because he knows I might get upset. I don't want to know all the gory details.

Toni: How did you feel the first time he told you about a date?

Mom: Lord, I didn't believe it! I always heard there were different people out there, but I didn't know they were that different. He's got enough stories to fill a book.

Basically, he's a good caring person. He's not some kind of bimbo out there on the street, doing all kinds of slimy stuff.

Dane: Mom, do you feel prostitution should be legalized? Because escorts fall under the category of prostitutes, and it's illegal.

Mom: You ain't lying, it's illegal. I was worried about that at first. But statistics are that very rarely a guy like Adrian will get busted.

But should it be legalized? With as many people as are doing it, I don't see why not. Because they're going to continue doing it, no matter what. Laws or no laws.

Dane: Mom, is there anything else you want to add about Adrian?

Mom: Yeah. It's not that I'm just his mother. He's my best friend.

We've always been able to talk. We have a good relationship. And I just can't judge him. Some parents don't have a very close relationship with their kids. I'm lucky that way. Adrian and I have always been close.

Into the Nineties

In 1991 Susan Faludi's book, *Backlash, The Undeclared War Against American Women* hit the best-seller list. Looking back over the eighties Faludi called those years "The backlash decade [that] produced one long, painful, and unremitting campaign to thwart women's progress." Faludi was not without hope, however. "And yet, for all the forces the backlash mustered," she wrote, "women never surrendered. The federal court may have crippled equal employment enforcement and the courts may have undermined twenty-five years of anti-discrimination law — yet women continued to enter the work force in growing numbers. Newsstands and airwaves may have been awash with frightening misinformation on spinster booms, birth dearths, and deadly day care — yet women continued to postpone their wedding dates, limit their family size, and combine work with having children. Television sets and movie screens may have been filled with nesting goodwives, but female viewers still gave their highest ratings to shows with strong-willed and independent heroines." Murphy Brown is Mary Tyler Moore's spiritual little sister.

The struggle began to pay off in the nineties. Women made headway on two fronts, economically and on gender-related issues.

At the beginning of the decade, sensational news stories moved three gender-related women's causes to the forefront of the nation's' consciousness. Rape, sexual harassment and domestic abuse came out of the shadows and claimed the spotlight.

Americans of both sexes were riveted to their television sets to follow the rape trial of William Kennedy Smith. Although Smith was acquitted, the message was clear: "Boys will be boys" was defensible no longer. The wealth and power that had shielded the peccadilloes of other Kennedy men from social approbation was powerless against the changing tide of public sentiment.

In the late summer of 1991 millions again were glued to their TV screens to watch the confirmation hearings of a justice of the Supreme Court accused of sexually harassing a female underling. Anita Hill's story of being intimidated and embarrassed by Clarence Thomas struck a painfully familiar chord with millions of working women. The senators on the committee had learned of the matter when Hill reported the incidents behind closed doors. But for a leak to the press, however, it would have been dropped. Reaction to the willingness of male lawmakers to turn a blind eye was overwhelming. Although the brouhaha did not block Thomas' confirmation, the message from the female constituency came loud and clear: Boys, you just don't get it.

In January of 1994, another sensational case burst into the headlines. Lorena Bobbitt was accused of cutting off her husband's penis after years of battering and marital rape. When the jury acquitted her, millions of women felt justice had been served. "Who could've imagined," shuddered *Esquire* magazine, "that seemingly reasonable women would one day go around high-fiving in the streets after the acquittal of a woman who'd cut off her husband's penis, taking the verdict not as merely one horrific wrong having neutralized another but as poetic justice itself?"

On the political front, in the aftermath of the Hill/Thomas hearings, more women (though still a tiny percentage) were elected to legislative office than ever before. Bill Clinton, running with his professional, outspoken and competent wife by his side, won the White House. His nomination, and the subsequent confirmation, of Ruth Bader Ginsburg to the Supreme Court virtually assured that Roe v. Wade would continue to guarantee women's reproductive freedom.

At the beginning of the nineties, women also made headway on the economic front. Women's earnings as a percentage of men's crept upward from sixty-five to seventy percent. The number of women in the professions in 1991, according to the U.S. Department of Labor, was equal to men. This group fared slightly better than the national average with earnings at seventy percent of men's. Nearly one-third of all small businesses in the U.S. were owned by women. According to two studies by the National Foundation of Women Business Owners, in 1992 there were an estimated 6.5 million women-owned businesses which employed more people in the U.S. than did Fortune 500 companies worldwide.

"Wealth of any kind, to any degree, is an expression of male sexual power," wrote feminist Andrea Dworkin in 1982. If that is true for men should it not be true for women? This question takes us back to our original purpose in writing this book. Why gigolos now?

Market Forces and the Return of the Gigolo

Undoubtedly, since the dawn of time there has been an abundant supply of men who'd be happy to be paid for doing what they best like to do. Only rarely, however, and in specific circumstances, do any of them get the chance. The *beaux* of England probably congratulated themselves on having been born in the right place, at the right time. Historically, only when women have had power, money and leisure time have they paid men to fulfill their more intimate needs.

Throughout most of history, as we've seen, only the aristocracy fit this picture. But in twentieth-century America, for the first time ever, we see a large affluent middle class that, in many ways, lives better than the the sultans of Persia. Yes, there are still enormous inequities in the relationship between men and women in America, but then everything is relative.

And relative to women in other parts of the world and women throughout history, American women are at the apex of privilege. Never in the history of the world have so many women employed so much power, held so much wealth and enjoyed such freedom.

In this country, the twenties was the first time that a substantial number of women had power to come and go as they pleased, money to spare, discretion over spending it and leisure time to devote to pleasure. It is no mere coincidence that gigolos sprang up then like truffles in the forest after a rain. When that era came to a halt with the Great Depression, gigolos disappeared from view. If there were any still around, and of course there must have been a few, no one cared to notice.

Until now.

Could it be that women's recent success is what's behind the resurgence of gigolos?

Why did they disappear so completely for so long?

Could it be that the tenor of the times then was wrong for gigolos, that women had more pressing matters on their social agenda? Or, were women holding out for the romantic ideal, earnestly believing that all that was need-ed to make it work between men and women was more fairness and com-munication, more love and understanding? Women and men today have experienced three decades of disillusionment on many fronts. Holding out for ideals may seem less reasonable than accepting flawed compromises.

Another puzzle: Unlike couples in the twenties when everybody knew what was going on, why are today's ladies so furtive about what they're doing, so bent on invisibility?

Are they afraid of the law? Sex for pay, whether the seller is a man or a woman, is prostitution and in most places it's illegal. Fear of the law, howev-er, is probably not a big factor because heterosexual male prostitution is almost never prosecuted. (In Las Vegas, interestingly, where female prostitu-tion is legal, the laws don't even address male escorts.) More likely, the stig-ma of prostitution is so deep-rooted for women that even when they are on the consumer, not supplier, side of the transaction, they feel compelled to secrecy.

Another key reason for secrecy is that in our culture, when a man keeps a woman, his status is enhanced; when a woman keeps a man, her status is diminished. People think, "Any woman can get laid. She must be a real dog if she has to buy a man."

Then why were the flappers so flagrant?

The answer is that the twenties were a more innocent time than the nineties. The relationship between flapper and gigolo was based on dancing or partying that might lead to more. The barter today is very different. Women now acknowledge their sexuality and believe that it's OK to ask for and get what they want. The deal between a woman and her hiree is openly money for services, specifically including sex. That's always a private transaction.

And where does AIDS fit in?

Apparently, at the half-point of the 90s, heterosexual men and women do not feel sufficiently threatened to give up fooling around. That's not sur-prising when you look at history. The fear of death has never stopped people from having sex, even brilliant people who knew better, who had the most to lose. The roster of famous victims of syphilis is impressive: the artist Eduard Manet, the great Beethoven and our own Ben Franklin, to name a few. Almost no one can be sure of being really safe today, anyway. Seventy percent of married men with annual earnings of sixty thousand dollars or more have had affairs. Is a woman married to a man who has a secret affair safer than one who hires a man and takes precautions?

The simplest and most plausible explanation for the resurgence of the American gigolo is that a large class of women today possess what men alone had for much of history: independence, money, and time to spend as they please. Women are simply doing what men have done for thousands of years — getting what they want by the most direct means, without a hassle, without having to explain.

Undoubtedly some women today, like many traditional men, don't want an equal partner; they want to be boss. We are again at one of those rare periods in history when circumstances conjoin to grant such women the ability to get what they want from men on their own terms. But that's not the whole story.

"Only recently," writes Nikki Finke in *Working Woman*, "has there been a significant number of successful women who made, rather than inherited, their money." For this class of women, finding a mate is not easy. Men marry younger women. When those marriages fail and the men remarry, they're likely to choose an even younger partner so there's a shortage of successful men in the pool with successful women. Of those who are around, few are secure enough to handle, let alone take pride in, a career-minded wife's achievements.

Women are conditioned to marry men more successful than they are. Rarely does it make financial sense for a woman to marry a man who is not, at least, at her level. When there are few Prince Charmings around, however, women settle for what is available. A woman will "keep" a man she'd never dream of marrying or engage a man as an armpiece for social functions, although she would never make a commitment to him.

Women today are sophisticated and critical. They've lived with men through the era of social disillusionments and add an additional disenchantment of their own. Many women are cynical about the "dream marriage" to "Mr. Right" their mothers envisioned for them. They see men as unwilling to meet them halfway (half the housework, half the child care, etc.) to make family life work. Male bashing is at an all time high. Two typical slogans have made the rounds: "If we can send a man to the moon, why can't we send them all there?" and "A woman needs a man like a fish needs a bicycle." The hostile climate in early 1994 was so pronounced that a *Time* magazine cover story featured a pig in a suit and tie with the caption, "Are men really that bad?"

For all the cynicism, women today know they are not fish and men are not pigs. And, as Madonna says, "Sex is not love and love is not sex." Women have worked hard at owning their sexuality, seeing themselves as deserving of receiving pleasure as much as being a pleasure object for a man. Women are not willing to sell their bodies and souls to "catch" a man. Better to have a man on their own terms, and money is often the key. Women are becoming more like men.

And men are becoming more like women. How many women reading these men's stories don't remember a time in their lives they've had sex with a man because it was part of what was expected? How many women can say they've never smiled and pretended to be interested when they were bored stiff? How many women marry men and stay with them and sleep with them after love is gone because it is financially advantageous? Will women see themselves as vastly different from the men in this book?

Christina

Christina answered an ad we had placed in the New Times paper in Ft. Lauderdale for women who had hired gigolos. We wanted to hear their stories. Promising Christina complete discretion, she agreed to a phone interview.

It took a lot of cajoling before she consented to speak with us. She asked us to call at a certain time when she knew her boyfriend would be gone. Caught between the fear of being discovered and her intense desire to tell someone about her double life, she finally gave in to her need to talk. She bared her soul to us, anonymous strangers who would listen and make no judgments.

Although Christina insisted that she has no emotional attachment to Danny, her glowing descriptions of his physical prowess and the special tone in her voice when she spoke about him indicate otherwise.

Toni: Tell us about yourself and how you met the escort you've been seeing.

Chris: OK. We both happen to live in the same condominium development. We had seen each other casually, and one day he approached me. He asked if I was married. I said I was living with someone. He said, "Does he work?" I said, "Yes, he does." He said, "You must be pretty bored." And I said, "Yes I am." He said, "Gee, I'll have to come and keep you company." I said, "That sounds very nice, I'd like that." He said, "Well, when is the next time your boyfriend works?" I said, "Tuesday." And so, the next Tuesday, exactly ten minutes after my boyfriend Phil left, there he was.

Toni: Do you work?

Chris: No.

Dane: Tell us about yourself.

Chris: I'm sixty-one years old, frosted blond hair, and everybody thinks I'm ten years younger than I am.

Toni: Can you give us a name that we can call the escort?

Chris: Well, I can't say his real name, so let's call him "Danny."

Toni: Describe Danny.

Chris: OK. I'm going to shock you now. I am white. This man is black. He is twenty-five years younger than me. I am 5 feet 2 inches, 107 pounds, he is 6 feet 3 inches, weighs 212 pounds. He is extremely good looking, comes from the Islands. The Barbados. He looks like a poster. He could be a movie star, he's so beautiful. And he's married.

Dane: He's married?

Chris: Yes. He didn't hide this from me. He has a child and right now his wife is three months pregnant. He married this woman after he found out she was pregnant with the first child, and they've stayed together because of the daughter. He loves that child very much. The relationship isn't too good. His wife might be a little worried, you know. I think she got pregnant this time to hold on to him because he does love his daughter and would never leave her.

Dane: Is he a professional escort?

Chris: Yes. For a number of years. He may see other women, I don't know. But I do know that the attraction I have to this man, it's something I never in a million years thought would take place. I was as shocked by it as you probably are. But there is something special there.

Dane: A chemistry?

Chris: Yes. Nobody has ever made me feel this way. Even when I was young. Even when I was married. And he can't believe how attracted he is to me either. He told me black women do not react like this. Their reaction is entirely different to men, and that he can't believe he has this effect on me.

Dane: What kind of reactions do black women have to him?

Chris: Typically they're very demanding. He says everything has to be their way. It's "Do this, do that" and "No, I don't like this, I don't want that." They don't appreciate a man. Plus he said he always was attracted to older women. In fact, he still thinks I'm ten years younger than I am! So I think if he ever knew how old I was he would probably have a heart attack.

Basically, we're friends too. But it turned out really funny. The physical part is absolutely fantastic, like something you'd see in a movie. Like you'd read in a book and you'd say, "Wow, wouldn't it be great if things were really like that?" It's the stuff you dream about.

Toni: What is a typical evening with him like?

Chris: Usually we spend two to three hours in bed.

Toni: Where do you meet?

Chris: Motels. We've met in empty apartments because he has a friend who's a maintenance man for the same apartment complex, so he can get keys. He comes to my house when my boyfriend goes to work.

We've even met in the bathroom at the pool. Mostly my place, though.

Toni: Do you give him gifts?

Chris: Yes, I've given clothes and cologne before, but one day he said, "In the future, if you ever give me anything, I'd like money."

Dane: How far into the relationship were you before he introduced the subject of money?

Chris: Maybe two or three weeks. The amount was never mentioned. After that he'd say, "Can I ask a favor of you?" And then it would be a certain amount of money he'd want for Christmas, or special occasions, or if we went to a motel. I would come right out and say to him, "What do you want?" He would say, "That's up to you." And sometimes he would tell me.

Toni: What did he want?

Chris: It varied. Sometimes a very small amount, two hundred or three hundred dollars. Sometimes he'd say he didn't want anything. Then he'd say five hundred dollars. Or one thousand dollars. Or he expected three thousand dollars for Christmas. Then the following week on New Year's he asked for one thousand dollars. It always varied.

There was no set rate. But I can't explain it. I'm not being charged to be made love to. I'm giving him the money. I actually want to give him the money.

Dane: Why, Christina?

Chris: Well, nobody has ever pleased me like this. Nobody has ever made me feel like this. He's not making me feel like he has to, like it's sickening or something. We just relax with each other. I feel he can be himself and I can be myself, and I'm getting what I want so I feel he should get what he wants, too.

Toni: What does he tell his wife when he's with you?

Chris: Sometimes he tells her he's out playing basketball. Other times he says he's working.

I've been in his car when the car phone rings. She has called him and he has told her something like some people in the development are leaving and they're throwing a party and don't expect him until late. While he was on the phone, he held his finger to his mouth so I'd be quiet, and

I just sort of looked the other way.

Dane: After he lied to his wife and hung up the phone, what was his reaction?

Chris: He apologized to me. He said it was embarrassing, and that he was sorry it happened. He's very much a gentleman, but I still felt uncomfortable.

Toni: The fact that he is married, does that ever bother you?

Chris: No. He told me, and I believe him, that he loves his wife. She loves him. But he also loves sex and she doesn't. And I happen to like sex.

He said when they did have sex, everything had to be her way. She found fault with everything he did rather than tell him she was getting enjoyment out of it.

Dane: How old is his wife?

Chris: Thirty-five. And he's thirty-six.

Toni: What would you say that you get from him that you don't get from your current relationship?

Chris: I have no sexual relationship at all with Phil. I was married to my first husband when I was nineteen. He passed away. A heart attack and cancer, and he was dead at forty-one.

Then I met Phil who was very handsome, a real playboy, full of fun and personality. We met in New York, and he asked me to come to Florida with him.

At that time he drank. I don't think he was an alcoholic, but he drank every day. When he drank, that was the only time we had sex. But he had a lot of inhibitions. Later he got sick and was told by a doctor he couldn't drink anymore. And then sex just stopped. He didn't want it at all.

With my husband, the sex was very good. But with Phil, the sex was a big let down. So I started going out with other men when the sex stopped between us.

When I used to work, I had affairs with people I worked with. Then when I stopped working, I stopped having sex for a period of three years because it wasn't as easy to meet men out of the workplace.

Dane: Three years?

Chris: When I met Danny, I hadn't had sex in three years. I said to him, "I'm really scared. Nervous. I haven't been with a man in three years."

Toni: So the man you live with, there is no sexual relationship at all?

Chris: No. In fact, we have an apartment with two bedrooms. I have one, he has the other. There is no affection, no sex, nothing. It's like we're roommates.

Dane: How long have you been with Phil?

Chris: Twenty years. He was extremely handsome at one time. He even modeled when he was younger. He used to party and drink, and when he drank, he was horny. Then all of a sudden he completely changed his looks, his clothes, his attitude. Now he acts like he's ready for a rocking chair.

Dane: How old is he?

Chris: Sixty, but he looks a lot older. My real age is sixty-one, and the man I'm seeing thinks I'm fifty-one. My doctor says I could easily pass for forty-seven.

Toni: Why would you choose to stay in a relationship for twenty years that was not rewarding for you sexually?

Chris: Different reasons. I have two daughters. They loved Phil. He treated them like they were his own. At the time I was working, having affairs on the side. I thought about leaving him but then my older daughter broke her engagement, had a nervous breakdown, and became anorexic. I was miserable and wanted out, and I told her as soon as she got back on her feet that I was going to leave. When we got her through that, she decided to go back to college. And she asked me if she could live here at home while she was in school. So again the timing didn't seem right. And then she didn't go out on her own until two years ago, and by then I had met Danny.

I don't want to move from here because then it would be very difficult for us to see each other. I mean, it's so convenient now. I leave my back door open, my front door open. I know when Phil comes and goes. He works six days a week.

Toni: Have you ever had any close calls? Has Phil ever found you and

Danny together?

Chris: Never. I know when Phil goes to work. I know exactly how long he'll be there. I know where he is at all times. If I'm going to a motel, I tell him I'm going shopping. He doesn't think anything of it. I'm careful, I don't go out in public with Danny.

Dane: Do you ever feel guilt about seeing Danny and living with your boyfriend?

Chris: No.

Dane: Do you ever feel yourself becoming emotionally attached to Danny?

Chris: It's the funniest thing. One day we were in a motel and Danny asked me if I was falling in love with him.

Toni: What did you say?

Chris: I said, "No. I love the way you make me feel. But as far as falling in love, no. You have your life; I have mine. I respect yours; you respect mine. I've chosen to stay where I am."

Toni: Christina, you seem interesting and attractive. Why would you choose to pay for an escort when you could probably go into any bar and find some man that would just love to be with you and would pay for everything for you?

Chris: First of all, I don't like the bar scene. To me, being picked up in a bar is different. With Danny, I was totally attracted to him from the first time I saw him. Instant chemistry. My first thought was, "Oh my God, I'd love to go to bed with this guy." I couldn't believe the way I felt.

When he saw me at the pool with my boyfriend that first time, he told me he had felt the same way. There was something between us, a definite chemistry.

Dane: When you had the first sexual encounter with Danny, after not having had sex for three years, can you describe in one word what it was like?

Chris: Unbelievable!

Toni: A lot of women have fantasies about being with a black male. Is it true that they are wonderful lovers?

Chris: Fantastic. Absolutely the best!

Toni: Better than white men, in your opinion?

Chris: Yes. This man was very large, very sensuous, passionate and gentle. He was considerate about pleasing me. And he says he can't believe the way I appreciate him and make him feel. As far as technique, I've never been made love to like this before. It seems to go on forever. I think we've done every position imaginable, in just about every place, and he never ceases to be wonderful!

Dane: What are some unusual places you've had sex?

Chris: Down at the pool, in the bathroom, on the sink. He had keys to empty apartments, and we'd do it on the floor of other people's apartments. The last time he was over, he brought a porno film and we did it on a reclining chair. We've done it on the kitchen counter.

As for positions, I think this guy is a contortionist!

Dane: Is he still as exciting after all this time?

Chris: If he walked through that door now, my heart would start pounding. I would start trembling.

And when I'm with him, there's no such thing as age or color. I don't think of myself as being twenty-five years older than him or that he's black. It's just, he's a man and I'm a woman.

Toni: There are some women that say that size doesn't matter. How do you feel about that?

Chris: Oh, yes it does. Absolutely. Positively. Definitely. I mean, the first time I saw him naked, I couldn't believe it. I said to him, "My God, you'll never fit on my waterbed. Take it easy!"

Toni: What would you say are some of the negatives to the relationship with Danny?

Chris: I don't always know if I can see him. I don't always know if he'll be able to come over. Or he'll have to rush off to his wife and his family. I've been waiting many times when he didn't show up. He couldn't. And he can't call me from his home.

Toni: How do you feel at the end of the evening when you've had this wonderful time, and he goes home to his wife?

Chris: I don't think about it. It's completely out of my mind. I just think about the time when we are together.

I have watched his daughter for him. She's the seven-year-old. She was here two weeks ago, and he had asked me if I would watch her when she had a day off from school and he had no place to bring her. He was working. She came here and spent the day.

Dane: Are you getting attached to her?

Chris: Yeah, I feel like she's my own little girl. She brings her bike or her roller skates. I love children, and she loves me. We have a good time together. And this seems to please her very much.

He told me that the reason he stays with his wife is because she said if they ever divorced, she would take the little girl from him and he would never be able to see her. And he loves this little girl so much. So he said he'd rather stay with his wife than lose his little girl.

Toni: Christina, the fact that you've been married before, that you've been in the wife's place, does that ever enter into your mind when you're with this man? Do you ever experience even a twinge of guilt regarding the wife?

Chris: No. I feel that if he was happy, he wouldn't need me. If he had the sex and affection at home, the appreciation, why would he be sleeping with someone else?

When I was married to my first husband, I never thought of going out or cheating on him. But this man that I'm living with does nothing for me. He has told me to go out and get myself a boyfriend. He said he doesn't want sex. He doesn't want affection.

Toni: Why do you think he's saying that? Why doesn't he want an intimate relationship?

Chris: I really don't know. One of his friends told me he has definite sexual hang ups. A lot of problems.

Dane: Have you suggested counseling?

Chris: Of course. He's promised to go over and over again, but nothing happens. You see, growing up he was told that sex is dirty. He was Catholic, and to him, you get into bed, leave your clothes on, wait until it's dark, the TV stays on. It's wam-bam, thank you, ma'am. And afterwards, the first words that are uttered are, "Go clean yourself quick." Because to him, it's a very dirty thing. The only reason to have sex is to procreate.

When he was younger, the only thing that made him have sex was the drinking. He'd lose his inhibitions. As far as oral sex, you don't even mention it! He looks like he'll get sick to his stomach if you suggest it.

I think I was born at the wrong time. When I was nineteen years old, I wanted to do all kinds of things. I was a trailblazer of sorts.

So to me, giving Danny money to do all the things that I enjoy and to please me, I feel, "Why shouldn't I give him the money?"

I hear my daughter talk about the bar scene. If you pick someone up, you don't know who he is. Is it going to be a one-night stand? How do you know this guy is even going to be any good in bed? Are you going to wind up somewhere saying, "Gee, I wish I wasn't here?" You just don't know what you're getting into. Danny is someone I know. I trust him. I like him.

Dane: How much money do you think you've spent on him in the time you've known him?

Chris: Over the two years I've been seeing him, thousands, I guess.

It's strange, too, because sometimes when he comes over, we make love three or four times. Yet he considers that as one session. So it's hard to average out.

Toni: What kind of gifts have you given him?

Chris: Clothing, mostly. Now I give him rum. He's from the Islands, Barbados. They drink this certain rum, and he just loves it. So I give that to him.

Toni: Christina, do you have any girlfriends that you talk to that know about your relationship with this male escort?

Chris: No. I have three good friends, but none of them would understand. I could never even mention it.

Dane: Your situation is unique, I think, because the man you're living with knows your escort, right? They both live in the same development?

Chris: Yes. My boyfriend even likes him. And Danny's been here. He's come in to do work, and my boyfriend even gave Danny a sweater for

Christmas! Just because he thinks he's such a hard-working guy. If he only knew! And when we're together, the three of us, I feel perfectly comfortable. It doesn't bother me a bit.

And I buy gifts for his daughter, too. Valentine's candy, things like that.

Dane: Do you think anyone in the development knows what's really going on?

Chris: No. I keep it very casual in public. Even when I watch his daughter, I make it very casual. People just think I'm a nice lady and that we're all just friends.

Never in a million years would my boyfriend think there's anything going on between us!

And it's funny because, even if my boyfriend is here, and Danny and I are pretending to be just friends, he'll still give me little special looks, squeeze my hand on the way out.

Toni: Do you think the secrecy of the relationship adds to the excitement?

Chris: Yes, definitely.

Toni: Christina, what advice would you have for another woman who's in a similar situation to you and wants to hire a male escort for the first time? What would you tell her?

Chris: I would say, "Go for it. Give it a try." If you had asked me a few years ago if I would ever be giving anybody money to make love to me, I would have said, "Not a chance!" I mean, I was always able to get men.

When I worked as a hostess, I was having an affair with my manager. All the other hostesses were young girls, yet I was the one who was seeing him. Younger men have always been attracted to me.

So what I'm saying is: I've never been in a position where I've even had to think of paying someone to go to bed with me. But yes, I'm doing it.

I mean, what am I going to do with the money? Frankly, I can't think of anything better to spend it on!

Toni: Do you think Danny would speak to us?

Chris: No. He told me, "Don't ever tell anyone about this."

Toni: If your boyfriend were to find out about your relationship with your escort, what do you think his reaction would be?

Chris: He'd throw me out of the house. I think he'd be shocked because this man was black. He'd call me everything under the sun! Yes, he told me to go find a boyfriend, but, in reality, he'd think I was a real slut to be with another man because he expects me to live like him.

In fact, when I was watching Danny's daughter, my boyfriend made a comment to me: "Why would you want to watch her? She's not even your daughter, and, on top of that, she's black."

I think he's very prejudiced. Seeing a white person and a black person together, he'd absolutely die. He'd have a heart attack. I've been with Phil for twenty years. I know how he thinks.

Dane: Twenty years is a long time to be going through such emotional pain.

Chris: Yes. Believe me, it's terrible.

Dane: Do you ever think about the day your affair with Danny will end?

Chris: Yes. I know one day it's going to end. First of all, I'm not getting any younger. And his wife is expecting a baby. And I think he may leave here and go back to school.

The only reason I'm staying here with Phil is because Danny's here. If he were to leave, I would leave and go someplace else. Once Danny leaves here, I don't think I'll ever see him again.

Toni: Does your boyfriend know about some of your other affairs?

Chris: Ah, he just asked me once if I'd ever had an affair and I said, "Yes, a long time ago." And that was it. He never asked me about it again.

Toni: If he were to find out about you and Danny, do you think Phil would be shocked by your sexuality?

Chris: Yes, he would be shocked. Because even when there's a sexy movie on TV, he just turns it right off. Calls the woman every kind of name going, pig, she's disgusting, on and on.

This sounds crazy, but I'd love to take a video of me and Danny and show it to Phil! When I leave him, and I am going to leave him, I'm going to tell him about Danny.

The thing is, even if he doesn't like sex, he should do something to satisfy me. But in his mind, I don't count.

Toni: Do you think that younger men are better lovers?

Chris: Definitely. Absolutely. When a man gets older, they worry that they can't please you. They have health problems, and so on. A younger man is very sure of himself. And Danny is totally ready at all times.

Toni: At what age do you think men start declining as lovers?

Chris: Well, I'd say men start declining sexually about the mid-forties. Then they start to have anxiety about themselves.

And it seems that most men think an older woman is a better lover. For example, Danny told me he met a girl once who was in her twenties, very beautiful, a figure you wouldn't believe. He couldn't wait to get to a motel room with her, and then he couldn't wait to get out of the motel room! She was so bad in bed, he said, so inexperienced and so unwilling. There was no passion, no feeling, no orgasm. With an older woman, he said, it's just the opposite. They're passionate, appreciative and wonderful.

And I can tell you, with Danny, I have multiple orgasms, so intense it's unbelievable. I mean, to have eight, ten, twelve orgasms is just incredible. And he experiences such pleasure out of giving me so much pleasure.

So the only way I would even consider staying with my boyfriend is if I could continue to have a relationship on the side with another escort. I might stay with him just because I'm getting older and don't want to be alone. At least, it's somebody to live with.

Toni: Does financial security factor in to your decision to stay with him?

Chris: Ah, yes, somewhat. I'm dependent on him because I don't work anymore, and I don't even have a car.

Dane: If this relationship with Danny were to end, would you call up an escort service?

Chris: Yes, I would. Definitely.

Dane: Even if you had to spend more money?

Chris: Yes, I would. As long as I could be as happy and content and satisfied as I am now.

Toni: Christina, there's sort of a stereotype about women who use escorts, that they're less attractive, that's why they have to pay for it, etcetera. What do you think about those stereotypes?

Chris: Oh, they're not true any more. I think there are a lot of women around, just like me, and they're just not admitting it. I think there are also women who wish they could be doing what I'm doing. I think there are plenty of women who would give anything to be in my shoes, to be with a man like Danny.

I talk to my friends. Their sex lives are terrible! A lot of them are younger, believe it or not, in their late twenties and early thirties. They have children and their husbands are ignoring them.

Dane: Do you think these younger women would pay for companionship?

Chris: Yes, I do. Because they will go out and spend a lot of money going out on the town with the girls and getting drunk just because they need a night out. I think they would rather spend their time with a man who paid attention to them and satisfied them.

The truth is there's a lot of women out there who are just like me, looking for someone. Needing someone. And having to pay for it just isn't that big a thing. It's totally worth it.

Toni's turn

The question I was asked most often during the course of working on this book was: What's it like to interview a gigolo? I think what they really meant, at least the women, was: Were they gorgeous? Were you attracted to any of them? Were they the fantasy, the movie version of American Gigolo?

Yes, some of them are extremely handsome, charming, and polished — excellent conversationalists who speak four languages and are outrageously attentive. And some seem to be quite average. They all dispense flattery at whim. The best trick is they make every woman feel special, as if she is the only one in the world who matters.

But then there were the others, the ones whose egos definitely worked overtime, who punctuated every sentence with "I, I, I." Then there were those who seemed angry at women, confusing sex with violence and abuse, and the ones who seemed broken, done in by a profession that crushes dreams, shatters illusions and forces its members to live in shadows and secrecy.

I found it interesting that they often had difficulty relating to me on a business level. Indeed, it seemed the only way they knew how to relate to women was in a sexual context. There were the ones who tried to bait me, and the ones who tried to flatter me, and the ones who tried touching my knee under the table! The more professional I was with them, the more they seemed perplexed, often bewildered, and, sometimes, I got the distinct impression they thought I was a challenge.

Perhaps the other most asked question was: Why write a book on gigolos?

We wrote the book out of curiosity, plain and simple. Why would a man choose to be a prostitute? Why would women choose to pay a man for sex? What was the emotional trade-off for these choices? And what kind of rewards did they get from this experience?

Of these questions, the reasons why women use gigolos most intrigued me. We spoke with the women directly. We asked the gigolos detailed questions about their clients, and we found that a large majority of women hiring escorts are intelligent, articulate, successful and attractive, a far cry from the picture society paints of a lonely and desperate woman. Indeed, they are often mothers, grandmothers, company presidents, maybe even the neighbor with the friendly smile down the street.

For many, it is simply a quick solution to an obvious problem — they want sex. Some women may be too busy to commit the time to a relationship or they may not want to make the emotional investment . They may want companionship, a friendly ear. For these women, a hired escort provides the perfect solution — an enjoyable evening with a handsome, charming companion with no strings attached.

Some women want to have a fantasy fulfilled. Perhaps it's the lure of the forbidden. They've always secretly wondered what it would be like to have another man. Or they want to try a unique sexual position or exotic role play-ing. Perhaps it is something that they cannot try at home. These women will pay to be swept off their feet, to make a fantasy come true. They look upon it as harmless fun.

For other women, the choice to use an escort appears more complicated. With women who are economically dependent on their husband, a control issue is sometimes at the core. Because they do not feel in charge of their home lives, they seek control elsewhere. By hiring an escort, by paying for sex, the situation is suddenly reversed. The woman now has the power, and the man finds himself in the position of having to please her.

Dane's turn

No one can precisely calculate how many men actually make their living as gigolos in the United States. But based on our research for this book, it seems as if there could be hundreds of thousands, from free lancers to men working for escort agencies in cities across the country. Prostitution no longer remains the domain of females walking midnight streets.

The breakdown of marriages in the eighties and nineties has created a built-in market for men with charm and physical attributes to make a liveli-hood by selling their unique brand of love and friendship for sometimes stagger-ing sums of money. Women, after going through failed relationships, sometimes find satisfaction and fulfillment in liaisons where they can maintain a level of control by paying for sex.

Who are these men, the gigolos? Although all the gigolos we interviewed were very different in terms of their social class, education and even their per-sonalities, there were some clear similarities between them. First, except for a couple who seemed to be angry, even dangerous people, most of the men appeared to like the women they serviced. Over and over we heard them describe one client or another as "a nice person."

Second, the men often referred to their desires to make the woman feel comfortable and to discover what she needed. This might be in terms of sex or even if she just needed to be held while she cried. They all seemed to consider that being a good listener was essential in this line of work and rarely expressed harsh or judgmental observations about their clients. Often they were very aware of the woman's feeling that she was not heard by the man in her life.

Third, while the average man who is not in the business prefers a certain "type" of woman, these guys all had the ability to be sexually aroused by just about anything female, regardless of age, weight, personality or looks.

Fourth, the escorts often mentioned their difficulties in maintaining a "normal" committed relationship. Whether this problem was the reason they got into the business in the first place or a result of it is hard to say. However, for all their ability to please a woman, they generally lacked whatever it is that's needed to make a long-term relationship work.

The moralities of the business bother some of them, but not most. The fear of AIDS looms large, but caution is often thrown to the wind. In the minds of these daredevils of sex with uncertain futures, all that matters is breathing the excitement and living on the edge.

Still, it does seem that there are a few lessons here for those of us non-gigolos who would like to improve our relationships with women.

What's in a Name?

Language is a funny thing. Without our realizing it, the words we use and the meanings we ascribe to them — and sometimes the words we don't use — reveal volumes about who we are.

Nowhere are the unconscious messages more ingrained than in the words that refer to gender roles. For instance, there are more than two hundred words that describe a prostitute or sexually promiscuous women (whore, tramp, slut, slattern, trollop, streetwalker, floozy, call girl, hooker, harlot, tart, etc., etc.) but only two words for the prostitute's customer (john, trick.) The words for the prostitute and the john are unbalanced; those for a prostitute are more pejorative than the ones for her customer.

In fact, word pairs that refer to men and women are often unequal. For instance, a governor is a highly-placed official, a governess is a domestic servant. The word "buddy," derived from baby-talk for "brother," means "a good friend." The word "sissy," derived from "sister" means a "coward or a wimp." Or, take "bimbo," generally understood as a beautiful armpiece, with air for brains. The male counterpart, a "hunk" or a "stud," is handsome but not air-headed. When *People* magazine calls John Kennedy, Jr. a hunk, he probably feels no inclination to sue.

An article in *Working Woman*, April, 1994, entitled "Trophy Husbands," referring to a successful woman's status-symbol spouse, immediately prompted a column from *The New York Times Magazine's* William Safire. "As a modern modifier," pronounced the illustrious word guru, "trophy most often means 'bimbonic' when applied to women, though a second sense remains of 'accomplished.' Applied to men, however, trophy is almost always complimentary."

In her book, *The Bias-Free Word Finder*, Rosalie Maggio refers to this phenomenon as semantic derogation. Words associated primarily with women undergo a depreciation over time so that two words, one male, one female, with the same root and same original message end up with very different meanings.

The pair master/mistress is a telling example. Both words come from the Latin *magister* (one who controls,) through Old French *maistre* (master) and *maistresse* (mistress.) The word mistress is the root for the titles, Miss and Mrs. which originally meant young woman and mature woman respectively. In current usage these titles indicate a woman's marital status. Master has not undergone a similar evolution; men are not labeled in relation to women.

Master has retained its meanings, "a man in authority, one who employs others or who has control over something." Think of all the ways we use this word: mastermind, masterpiece, masterwork, master plan, master class, masterful, master bedroom.

Mistress, too, has kept as primary those powerful meanings: "a woman who rules or has control, a woman in authority or power, a woman who employs others in her service." The *Oxford Dictionary* even gives "having the upper hand." So far so good; the pair is balanced.

Now try this exercise. Say, "He was her master." No doubt about who's the boss here.

Now try, "She was his mistress." No doubt about who's boss here either, and it isn't the woman. A mistress is "kept" by a sugar daddy (who is rich, powerful, maybe has a diamond pinky ring and big cigar).

Now try this:

A gigolo is kept by a _____.

Or, let's go back to our first example: Prostitute, the seller of a service and john, the buyer. What about:

Paid escort, the seller and _____, the buyer.

That's right. We have NO word in the English language for the female buyer of a man's sexual services. What does this missing word tell us about ourselves?

Ask Steven Pinker, MIT professor and author of *The Language Instinct: How the Mind Creates Language*, and he says, "Language does not shape thought; it's the other way around. We coin words when we need them. When we don't have a word for something, it's because we've had no occasion to coin one."

Because we've never conceived of a woman as the more powerful half of a sexual relationship, we've never needed a feminine word for this role. Naming is power. In the darkest form, oppressors name the oppressed: Early explorers called the native peoples they encountered "savages." Heterosexuals called homosexuals "queers." What does it tell us that there are over two hundred deprecating names for a prostitute and two rather neutral ones for a john?

In the brightest form, people name themselves: Homosexual men named themselves "gay." "Physically challenged" people rejected being called "the disabled" and named their athletic event the "Special" Olympics. Feminists discarded the honorifics "Miss" and "Mrs." in favor of "Ms." for both.

But women who pay for men's sexual services have not named themselves. Is a female "john" a "joan" or a "jane?" Is a "trick" a "trickess?" This nomenclature parallels a particular way men use women — wham, bam and impersonal. In fact, women's relationships with the men they pay are usually more complex, more like a man with a mistress.

Men who were named gigolos, today call themselves escorts. Another possibility: they might also be called "kept men." In contrast with the broad array of words that describe women who sell their sexual services, there is a dearth of words that describe the range of roles played by a "man who lives off a woman's money" (Ferber's definition).

The possibilities are limitless. He may offer a fantasy-fulfilling one-night-stand or a long-running erotic friendship. He may be a live-in sexual attendant, a Platonic companion, or an occasional escort for business or social events. In some cases, the line may blur as to whether he's her gigolo or her unemployed boyfriend. One distinction is clear, however. With a gigolo, the woman has both money and control; the relationship is on her terms.

What is the female equivalent of a sugar daddy? Pinker suggests "sugar mama" because it is easily understood as the feminine of sugar daddy and has a warm feeling to it. Maggio suggests "Ms. Got-Rocks" which connotes assertiveness through the alternate meaning "woman who has balls." Mistress, in its primary meaning "woman in control" has the right meaning but the word carries baggage. Perhaps the way to take back the word is to follow the example of the feminists who took back "mistress" with the title, "Ms." Try this:

A gigolo is kept by a Ms. Tress.

As language reflects changes in society, people will continue to name themselves and others in ways that define their relative power. Madonna, today's blond sex symbol, is not the vulnerable, dim child-woman that Marilyn Monroe was; she represents the ultimate expression of "woman in control." Photos often show her surrounded by her "boy toys." Perhaps it is a sign that men and women are truly becoming equal that William Safire has dignified in his column the first male equivalent of "bimbo": stud muffin.

D.M.

LIST OF REFERENCES

Balsdon, J.P.V.D. *Roman Women: Their History and Habits.* Westport, Connecticut: Greenwood Press, 1962.

Beauvoir, Simone de. *Le Deuxième sexe.* Paris: Gallimard, 1978.

Colacello, Bob. "Doris Duke's Final Mystery," *Vanity Fair,* March 1994, pp. 136-145; 170-176.

Croutier, Alev Lytle. *Harem: The World Behind the Veil.* New York: Abbeville Press, 1989.

Erenberg, Lewis. *Steppin' Out.* Chicago and London: The University of Chicago Press, 1981.

Faludi, Susan. *Backlash: The Undeclared War Against American Women.* New York: Doubleday, 1991.

Ferber, Edna. *Gigolo.* Garden City, New York: Doubleday, Page and Co., 1922.

Jonas, Gerald. *Dancing: The Pleasure, Power and Art of Movement.* New York: Harry N. Abrams Inc., 1992.

Madonna. *Sex.* New York: Warner Books, 1992.

Maggio, Rosalie. *The Bias-Free Word Finder.* Boston: Beacon Press, 1991.

Maggio, Rosalie. *The Nonsexist Word Finder.* Phoenix, Arizona: Oryx Press, 1987.

Moats, Alice-Leone. *The Million Dollar Studs.* New York: Delacorte Press, 1977.

Montesquieu. *Les Lettres persanes.* Paris: Garnier Frères, 1960.

Orlandi, Enzo. *The Life and Times of Louis XIV.* Philadelphia and New York: The Curtis Publishing Co., 1967.

Penzer, N.M. *The Harem.* Philadelphia: J.B. Lippincott Co., 1937.

Ramsey, Lynn. *Gigolos: The World's Best Kept Men.* Englewood Cliffs, New Jersey, Prentice-Hall, Inc., 1978.

Shulman, Irving. *Valentino.* New York: Trident Press, 1967.

Vaussard, Maurice. *Daily Life in Eighteenth Century Italy.* New York: The MacMillan Co., 1963.

Walker, Alexander. *Rudolph Valentino.* Briarcliff Manor, New York: Stein and Day, 1976.

Wolf, Naomi. *The Beauty Myth.* New York, 1991.

NOTES

p. 12. "...period when women..." Walker, A.

p. 13. "There were many establishments..." Shulman, I.

p. 13. "...put almost any woman..." Shulman, I.

p. 13. "...in their emancipation..." Shulman, I.

p. 53. "real monster..." Moats, A-L.

p. 81. "...woman was his mistress..." Ramsey, L.